CONCILIUM

concilium 1992/6

THE DEBATE ON MODERNITY

Edited by
Claude Geffré and
Jean-Pierre Jossua

SCM Press · London

Copyright © 1992 Stichting Concilium
English translations © 1992 SCM Press Ltd

All rights reserved. No part of this publication may be reproduced, stored in a retrieval system, or transmitted, in any form or by any means, electronic, mechanical, photocopying, recording or otherwise, without the prior written permission of Stichting Concilium, Prins Bernhardstraat 2, 6521 AB Nijmegen, The Netherlands.

December 1992

ISBN: 0334 03017 x

Typeset at The Spartan Press Ltd, Lymington, Hants
Printed by Mackays of Chatham, Kent

Concilium Published February, April, June, August, October, December

Contents

Editorial   Towards a Theological Interpretation of Modernity
   Claude Geffré and Jean–Pierre Jossua   vii

I · The Historical Destiny of Modernity   1

Modernity: A Sociological Perspective
   Gregory Baum   3

Catholicism and Modernity: A Process of Mutual Exclusion
   Emile Poulat   10

The Philosophical Critique of Modernity
   Helmut Peukert   17

Attempts at Reconciling Modernity and Religion in Catholic
and Protestant Theology
   Christoph Theobald   27

II · Postmodernity: Its Seductions – and a Critique   37

The End of Enlightenment: Post-Modern or Post-Secular?
   John Milbank   39

Between Praxis and Theory: Theology in a Crisis over
Orientation
   Werner Jeanrond   49

The Reciprocal Exclusiveness of Modernity and Religion
among Contemporary Thinkers: Jürgen Habermas and
Marcel Gauchet
   Anne Fortin-Melkevik   57

III · The Crisis of Modernity and the Church's Attitudes   67

What is Christian about Europe?
   Rudolf von Thadden   69

The Debate about Modernity in the North Atlantic World
  and the Third World
    JUAN CARLOS SCANNONE   78
The Attitude of the Church to the Modern World at and
  after Vatican II
    GIOVANNI TURBANTI   87
The Strategies of Reconquest in the New Europe and the
  Impossibility of Getting Past Secularization
    JEAN-LOUIS SCHLEGEL   97
Opportunities for the Christian Message in Tomorrow's World
    PAUL VALADIER   107
'Post-Marxism' and 'Post-Modernity': What is the Church's
  Presence?
    PAUL BLANQUART   115

Special Column   Correspondence in Communion   124

Contributors   127

Editorial: Towards a Theological Interpretation of Modernity

'Modernity' and 'post-modernity' have become the key words in a debate characteristic of the end of this century. As could have been foreseen, this debate is of immediate relevance to the very destiny of Christianity in the contemporary world. What is at stake is no less than the future of Christianity in a society undergoing a change from 'modernity', a change described by the extremely problematical expression 'post-modernity'. The debate is not only historical or sociological; it is also specifically theological. Far from always being interpreted in terms of a challenge, modernity could well be an opportunity for Christianity. So the present issue of *Concilium* must be approached as a kind of inventory of modernity with a view to its theological reinterpretation.

A sociological approach could describe modernity as the new civilization inaugurated at the end of the eighteenth century by two major events: the industrial revolution and the democratic revolution. But that is no more than a *description* of modernity. If we want to discover the roots of the specific dynamic of modernity, we will hardly go wrong in referring to the concepts of subjectivity and rationality. The transition to modernity coincides with the emergence of a human subject aware of its autonomy and with the victory of a rational analysis of all the phenomena of nature and society (including scientific progress, industrial processes, the development of a world economy and the bureaucratic centralization of the modern state). And now we have the fascinating awareness of how Christianity and modernity are both akin to and distanced from each other, in the double form of an inviolable subjectivity and a triumphant rationality.

The best-known version of the relationship between Christianity and modernity is the view that they are mutually exclusive. Western Christianity sought to be resolutely anti-modern where it felt that Enlightenment reason had undermined the authority of revelation and tradition and where the advent of democratic societies was a direct challenge to the hierarchical principle of the church as a society. Intransigent Catholicis was the historical response which sought to maintain the integrity of the Christian tradition in the face of the sacrilegious claims of modernity. After a long period of experimentation punctuated by regular attempts at restoration, with Vatican II it at last proved possible to make some distinctions and to understand that secularization is not necessarily to be identified with a secular atheism, that freedom of conscience would not fatally compromise the rights of a true objectivity, and that the separation of church and state could be the best guarantee of freedom of speech for believers.

However, now that the vague concept of 'post-modernity' is seeking to contain a degree of crisis in modernity bound up with the decline in the ideologies of progress and scientism, the collapse of Marxism and the reconstitution of the concept of reason, we are being invited to try a new interpretation of the relationship between modernity and Christianity. It has been discovered that Christianity was a 'vector' of modernity, though it finally became modernity's 'victim'. Modernity is said to be the development of potentialities inherent in Christianity (in particular the emergence of the human subject as an agent of history) which are said to have produced the modern world. And when this modern world had in fact incarnated all the potentialities of Christianity, it became the ever more powerful rival of Christianity as a historical force. Hence, at the present time, the destiny of a Christianity which has lost its power to provide social cohesion can be interpreted, within modernity, as being a progressive and inescapable disappearance. Some interpreters have even felt able to write that Christianity is the religion 'of the departure from religion'.

Still, it has yet to be demonstrated that the end of the social function of religion necessarily involves the end of religion as an experience and a belief. That demonstration is possible only if one decrees *a priori* that the essence of the religious is to be found at the origins of humanity and is to be defined as a total submission to the divine and to the immutable order of the universe. Now it seems that the truly religious is not exhausted in its functions of holding together a social group, or having a humanizing effect on individuals. If Christianity played a decisive role in the bringing to birth of modernity understood as the advent of free and autonomous subjects, that is not because it has betrayed the essence of religion, but rather because it inaugurated a radical dis-alienation from religion experienced in terms of the free response of human beings to the free gift of God.

It has become a commonplace to say that since the eighteenth century relations between the church and modern society have been relations of conflict, the inevitable conflict between the authority of a reason come of age and the authority of a church clinging tightly to its ancient privileges. But it is less commonplace to affirm that this particular historical configuration is not normative for the future and that the current crisis of modernity is forcing us seriously to question whether religion and modernity are necessarily exclusive.

This alleged crisis of modernity continues to be the object of a variety of interpretations. This issue of *Concilium* has tried largely to reflect these interpretations from the various geographical spheres of theology. At the same time, however, we believe that we can detect a broad consensus on two convictions. First, what it is convenient to call postmodernity does not in any way put in question the irreversible gains of modernity, specifically the critical vigour of the historical method, the autonomy of culture, the uncoupling of religion and politics, the legitimacy of the modern state as a legal state, and the legitimate autonomy of civil societies in the name of democratic reason. On the other hand, we do not want to yield to the temptation of explaining a return of religious interests in the West in terms of a failure of the ideals of modernity. It is, rather, the reconstitution of modernity within itself which can both explain the new relevance of the religious and encourage an unprecedented negotiation between modernity and Christianity.

The new credibility of the religious in the contemporary world can be interpreted as an expression of modernity itself, if by modernity one does not just understand a certain historical figure of Western man, which coincided with the industrial revolution, the phenomenon of secularization and the advent of democratic societies. Modernity (which persists in the era of postmodernity) also denotes the myth of the indefinite change of human beings who are aiming at the limitless fulfilment of their possibilities. Contrary to a somewhat hasty judgment, we would then understand why the massive phenomenon of secularization in the West does not tell against some return of the religious.

Thus post-modernity, far from denoting a return to the past which would satisfy the aspirations of those eternally nostalgic for anti-modernity, would above all denote the limit of a reason which is too sure of itself. In fact it seems that our era has a more vivid awareness of the limits of so-called instrumental reason, despite its amazing conquests in the sphere of economics and technology, and is in search of a more essential rationality which takes on the theoretical, practical and ethical, aesthetic, and even religious components of human thought. And then the new audience for the great religions of the world, which still surprises those observers who are heirs of the Enlightenment, can bear witness to this irreducibility of the religious being, who cannot be defined adequately as a being with needs or as a place of exchanges, but is also a being with a desire and aspiration for an *otherness*.

It is already a long time since the postmodern thinkers denounced the drift of reason magnified by the Enlightenment; a reason the instrumental scope of which is exhausted; a reason which has a direct link with the typically modern hybris of political power that goes under the name of totalitarianism. Those liberal societies which obey the logic of the multiplication of needs and their satisfaction run the risk of becoming shut in on themselves and of bringing into being the era of the void, of anonymity and protective individualism. It would truly be the destiny of another regime of reason, that of 'communicational reason', to encourage the advent of an open and perpetually autogenetic society, in the name of the democratic debate and the quest for a truth which can never be decided. Surely we cannot fail to detect a secret affinity between this new modernity and Christianity as a religion of the word communicated and shared, as a religion of otherness, and openness to what it lacks?

There is surely a need to rethink creatively the new forms in which the church can be present and can communicate in the post-modern and post-Marxist societies of a new Europe which is in search of itself. This is one of the promising tasks of a theological interpretation of modernity. And several articles in this issue bravely seek to analyse the challenges and the opportunities of the Christian message in the face of the modernity of the twenty-first century.

Beyond the different sensibilities one can see a real consensus in the rejection of the illusory dream of a new 'Catholicization' of Europe. As a partner of pluralist and democratic societies, the church cannot claim to recapture a dominant position. But for all that, it cannot allow itself to be progressively marginalized. Certainly, it can no longer intervene as though it exercised a kind of moral *magisterium* to a lay society thought to lack any ethical demands. However, it would be unfaithful to its prophetic vocation if it forbore to bear witness to its vision of human beings and society. The existence of a secular ethic which largely coincides with the ethics of human rights and which is commonly accepted by our liberal societies does not in any way make superfluous the witness borne to the paradox of the gospel.

In a Europe which risks becoming a mercantile Europe, the gospel reminds us of the dignity of all those whom society forgets. As the repository of the message of the Beatitudes, the church has a vocation to bear witness to the preferential love of God for the poor and those without rights. Furthermore, in the face of rising nationalisms, religious fanaticisms and antisemitism, in this multicultural and multireligious Europe, the gospel respect for the stranger is more topical than ever. Finally, one of the major challenges of this last decade of the twentieth century, in Europe as in the rest of the world, is the growing domination of economic technology which is invading all the spheres of our social and cultural life and of the media. Can modern men and women master their own power, or better the effects of their power on human life and on the future of the planet Earth? The historic vocation of Christianity – and it is a vocation which it shares with Judaism – would be an authoritative wisdom which recalled men and women to their *sabbatical* vocation.

Claude Geffré
Jean-Pierre Jossua

I · The Historical Destiny of Modernity

Modernity: A Sociological Perspective

Gregory Baum

Sociologists tend to define modernity as the civilization initiated in the late eighteenth century by two major societal events, the industrial revolution and the democratic revolution. These dramatic institutional changes produced and promoted a new culture. The industrial revolution created great wealth, multiplied the impact of capitalism on society, and generated two new social classes: the owners of the industries, the new ruling class, and the working class. It also created the modern metropolis. It promoted the development of science and technology and generated the expectation of unending progress.

The democratic revolution, independent of industrialization and yet in many ways related to it, also had an enormous cultural impact. It rejected the traditional hierarchies, promoted the ideals of freedom and equality, and generated among the bourgeoisie, and eventually also among the people, the desire for political participation. At the same time, paradoxically, democracy created the modern state characterized by the centralization of power and an ever-expanding bureaucracy.

The two revolutions embodied ideas derived from seventeenth- and eighteenth-century Enlightenment thought that rejected traditional values and institutions and looked upon reason as the organ of human self-liberation. Reason here referred to demonstrable science to understand and control nature and society; reason also referred to rational philosophy that defined human destiny in terms of freedom and responsibility.

The new world in the making generated responses among the different sectors of European society that introduced a new political vocabulary.[1] The people who created the revolutions, welcomed the cultural transformation, and trusted reason as guide to human progress were 'the liberals', strongly represented among the rising bourgeoisie. The success of industrial capitalism and political democracy eventually made 'liberalism' the dominant philosophical stance in modern societies. But there were people who lamented the arrival of modernity and tried to prevent it from spreading: these were 'the conservatives'. In the defence of traditional values, conservatives were often inventive and produced original ideas: that is why conservative thought must be understood as part of modernity.[2] Another reaction to the emerging modern society was found among 'the radicals'. With the liberals they affirmed social transformation and progress guided by reason, but with the conservatives they lamented many of the results of modernization. Famous among the radicals were 'the socialists', who argued that the revolutionary transformation of society had not gone far enough and that democracy was an empty promise if it did not include the democratization of the economic order.

The nineteenth- and early twentieth-century thinkers who studied the emergence of the modern world and compared it with the old, feudal-aristocratic society, produced a critical literature that generated the science of sociology. These thinkers (Durkheim, Fustel de Coulange, Le Play, Marx, Simmel, Tocqueville, Tönnies, Weber) were sensitive to the dark side of the industrial and democratic revolutions. In one way or another, they all recognized that industrial capitalism and liberal democracy undermined social solidarity, encouraged individualism, reduced all values to utility, and fostered a universal relativism. The young Marx lamented 'the alienation' inflicted upon humans, preventing them from assuming responsibility for their political and economic institutions, Durkheim sorrowed over 'the anomie' produced in wide sectors of the population through the decline of community and the cult of the individual, and Weber deplored 'the rationalization' of human existence through the ever-increasing spread of technology and bureaucracy.

Modernity and religion

In Europe, the entry into modernity was accompanied by secularization. Religion now had to prove its usefulness within the categories produced by the rationalization of society. Since new, secular myths, derived from the Enlightenment, now defined the destiny of society, religion lost an important function it exercised in the past. The new social classes, *viz.* the bourgeoisie and the proletariat, found religion of little use. Religion remained strong in the pre-modern social classes: the aristocracy, the artisans, the small merchants, the peasants, and in general among conservatives attached to traditional society. The Catholic Church identified itself with the conservative sector of European society and opposed the spread of modernity wherever it could.

Many sociologists have argued that the new trust in science and the cultural power of rationality inevitably led to the waning of religion. Some sociologists praised the growing reliance on scientific reason and the overcoming of religion (Auguste Comte), while others lamented that the increasing rationalization of society produced 'the disenchantment of the world' (Max Weber), the decline of religion and the obsession with material progress.

Yet the arguments that science and technology produce a culture hostile to religion are not wholly convincing, since they do not account for the historical experience of the United States of America. Tocqueville visiting America in the 1830s was amazed how faithful Americans were in their religious practice. He recognized that voluntaristic, pluralistic, denominational religion, so different from the European tradition, exercised important social functions in American society, providing people severed from their European origins and constantly on the move in a large country with a strong sense of community and with access to values that could correct the restlessness of American life. Subsequent sociological studies have demonstrated that even as social patterns were shifting, religion continued to exercise important social functions in American society, even if a high percentage of intellectuals remain aloof from it.[3]

The impact of modernization on religion remains an open question. There is no evidence, for instance, that in parts of South-East Asia that have become highly industrialized, such as Hong Kong, Singapore, South Korea and Taiwan, religion has suffered a decline.[4] One might even argue that the arrival of modernization in the various regions of Asia and Africa has intensified people's attachment to their religious traditions. While these people look upon a degree of industrialization as a necessity and find democratic institutions attractive, they want to avoid assimilation to Western culture. As they open themselves to the modernizing processes, they often rely on their religious tradition to keep them from losing the cultural continuity with their own past.

The complexity of modernity

Modern civilization, defined by industrialization and democracy, is a complex historical reality. It includes the dominant liberal trend. In the Anglo-American world, John Locke's liberal political philosophy remains culturally influential to this day, legitimating democracy, defending personal freedom and minimal government, and blessing the capitalist venture. But Marxism was part of modernity too. It also embraced the rationalistic illusion of necessary progress. Yet from the beginning, because of the many levels in European society, Enlightenment rationalism and the emergence of modernity were accompanied by critical intellectual, cultural and social movements. I have already mentioned the emergence of conservative thought. Of great importance was the Romantic reaction to the Enlightenment which produced new insights and values: a new, self-reflective inwardness, the appreciation of experience, the cognitive dimension of feelings, the respect for honest self-articulation, suspicion in regard to truths that claim universality, and the rootedness of personal experience in a historical context. The Romantic movement is part and parcel of modernity: its insights and values continue to shape present-day culture.[5]

The crisis of modernity

Around the turn of the century Max Weber, accompanied by other German intellectuals, came to believe that the rationalizing trend of modernity, the cultural power of instrumental reason, was so overwhelming that it would eventually overcome all counter-trends in society, produce an inflexible, oppressive, scientifically programmed society, 'the iron cage', accompanied by cultural decline and the death of all truly human dreams. According to Weber, this was the end of utopia. He believed that any counter-movement, inspired by an alternative vision, would succumb to rational organization, technical reason and bureaucratic control, and end up promoting the same programmed society. He predicted the dictatorship of the bureaucrats. (Weber's contribution to sociology was much richer than his theory of decline. It is even possible to argue against this theory by drawing upon other aspects of Weber's thought.)

After the First World War, many people asked themselves if the Enlightenment had not been a terrible mistake and if modern, industrial society was not operating out of a paradigm of rational control that would reify human existence and thus ultimately destroy it. These fears were expressed by existentialists and phenomenologists: they responded to it by questioning the primacy assigned to scientific knowledge. The same fears were expressed by populist and later by Fascist movements that promoted a post-bureaucratic, post-rational, communal society, hostile to the emancipatory thrust of the Enlightenment.

The social philosophers of the Frankfurt School gave an important answer to these questions.[6] They agreed with Max Weber that the increasing power of instrumental reason was dehumanizing society, but they refused to join the thinkers who rejected the Enlightenment legacy altogether. As critical heirs of the Marxist tradition the Frankfurters passionately defended as a demand of reason itself the emancipation of all human groups from the structures of exclusion and contempt and the heavy burdens placed upon their shoulders.

The Frankfurters recognized that over time the Enlightenment had become an obstacle to human emancipation. Originally Enlightenment rationality embodied a twofold thrust: instrumental reason dealing with science and technology, and substantive or practical reason dealing with human destiny and human freedom. But in the course of the nineteenth century, the Frankfurters argued, Enlightenment rationality collapsed into instrumental reason alone. The urgent task of the present, after recognizing the dark side of the Enlightenment, was not to reject it altogether, but instead to struggle for a cultural retrieval of substantive reason as a source of ethics, and simultaneously to denote instrumental reason from its cultural dominance. Against existentialists and phenomenologists the Frankfurters defended the importance of the natural sciences, and against populists and Fascists, they defended emancipation and solidarity as the uniquely human destiny. The Frankfurt School called their own critique of the Enlightenment 'dialectical', involving negation and retrieval, and opposed as dangerous for the human community any non-dialectical negation of the Enlightenment.

Has modernity come to an end?

In recent decades so many changes have taken place in Western capitalist society that some sociologists have wondered if the social reality still fits into the categories of modernity. They argue, for instance, that the ownership of the large industries has been distributed over vast numbers of shareholders and that thus the owners no longer constitute the ruling class. Power is now exercised by high-salaried technical experts, scientists or engineers, who run the industries in a rational manner, not to maximize profits but to achieve steady and reliable performance. At the same time the workers and employees of these industries belong to so many different levels of competence and thus of remuneration that it no longer makes sense to speak of a working class. Society, these sociologists say, has become post-industrial.

Daniel Bell has offered a rose-coloured reading of this post-industrial society.[7] Gone, he believes, are class oppression and class struggle, gone are the endless ideological debates. The problems of society have now become purely technical: they can be resolved by technical experts relying on objective science, technological know-how, and administrative reason. Post-industrial society creates a new space, Bell believes, for the exploration of human meaning and personal happiness.

A more realistic account of post-industrial society is given by Alain Touraine, who also observes that industrial owners and industrial workers no longer constitute economic classes and that power is now exercised by technical experts in the bureaucracies of industry, government, and all large organizations. No longer is the working class the special victim of alienation: post-industrial society inflicts alienation upon a much wider range of citizens. Touraine makes brilliant use of this analysis to explain the emergence of the new social movements – ecological movements, peace movements, women's movements, cooperative movements, movements to save the cities, movements promoting solidarity with the Third World, and so forth. The class struggle is being displaced, in part at least, by the struggle of the citizens against the bureaucracies.[8]

While I find in Touraine's analysis much that is convincing, I think it is misleading to designate contemporary society as 'post-industrial'. It is misleading because the institutional and cultural consequences of industrial capitalism are still with us: the trust in the logic of market, the reliance on instrumental reason, and the utilitarian anthropology.

Certain philosophers have claimed that Western society is moving into the post-modern age. Some argue that the Holocaust was an epiphany of dread that revealed the illusory nature of reason, emancipation and humanity. This argument deserves serious attention. Emil Fackenheim speaks to this in his book, *To Mend the World*.[9] According to him, those insights and commitments remain valid for the post-Holocaust world that during the Holocaust were sustained by the victims and that sustained them. He tells his readers of the great souls who resisted the reign of terror thanks to their reliance on human reason or religious faith. In fidelity to them, we dare not abandon the human vocation.

What is perhaps more important is that most post-modern philosophers had at one time embraced Marxism with its theory of historical necessity. After they recognized the totalitarian nature of the communist regimes, they repented of their past and loudly proclaimed 'la fin des grands récits', the collapse of all meta-stories or secular myths, Marxist and liberal, that pretended to interpret the entire course of history. Since the post-modern thinkers identify these myths with modernity, they now hail the arrival of the post-modern age. What has become discredited, they argue, is the Enlightenment notion of universal reason. It was a modern illusion, they continue, to think that people could become agents of emancipation and assume responsibility for their social world. This is no common history, they say: there is only a plurality of groups and communities, each relying on their own traditions, without a common logos that would enable them to engage in dialogue and cooperation.

Is it useful to call these theories post-modern? As I have indicated in this article, modernity is a complex historical reality including from the beginning critiques of Enlightenment reason – think of Rousseau, think of Kierkegaard – that did not urge a return to the past but opened up new spheres of reflection. What has been named post-modern is a phase of modernity itself.

In his book *La condition postmoderne*, Jean-François Lyotard offers a sociological interpretation of the entry into the post-modern age.[10] He holds that present-day capitalism, having achieved self-perpetuating stability, has transcended its own historicity. Organized in giant transnational corporations, the world economy is guided by management teams that operate on purely technical, value-free, scientific grounds. The world economic system, geared toward maintaining and improving its performance, no longer has a historical subject. Neither persons nor groups of persons nor governments are able to assume responsibility for its orientation. The economy has become subjectless.

Living under this transcendent, industrial, computerized dome, people discover that the Enlightenment notion of reason, history and emancipation are total illusions. Delivered from historical responsibility, they are now free to explore forgotten or repressed aspects of their lives, rejoice in singularity and in pluralism, and create networks of the like-minded who together resist the pressures of uniformity imposed on them by the transcendent iron dome.

Lyotard's post-modern theory stands or falls with his analysis of contemporary capitalism. Though a brilliant caricature, his analysis cannot account for the conflicts between the European, American and South–East Asian economies nor for the deadly irrationalities capitalism is producing in the human community, not least among them the multiplication of the poor, the homeless and the hungry.

We are still, I conclude, in the civilization created by industrialization and democracy, still caught in the clash between contradictory forces, the domination of instrumental reason with its dehumanizing consequences and the movements of resistance based on the conviction, be it secular or religious, that humanity has an ethical vocation.

Notes

1. Robert Nisbet, *The Sociological Tradition*, New York 1966, 9–16.
2. Karl Mannheim, *Konservatismus*, ed. David Kettler et al., Frankfurt 1985.
3. See the most recent study, Robert Wuthnow, *The Restructuring of American Religion*, Princeton 1988.
4. *The Changing Face of Religion*, ed. James Beckford and Thomas Luckmann, Newbury Park, CA 1989.
5. Charles Taylor, *Sources of the Self: The Making of the Modern Identity*, Harvard 1989.
6. See 17–26 below.
7. Daniel Bell, *The Coming of Post-Industrial Society*, Harmondsworth 1976.
8. Alain Touraine, *The Self-Production of Society*, Chicago 1977; *The Voice and the Eye*, Cambridge 1981.
9. Emil Fackenheim, *To Mend the World*, New York 1982.
10. Jean-François Lyotard, *La condition postmoderne*, Paris 1979.

Catholicism and Modernity: A Process of Mutual Exclusion

Emile Poulat

It is generally accepted that the Catholic Church condemned and rejected modernity with an inflexible intransigence, at least up to Vatican II. Hence the historical model which Italian historians were the first to call 'intransigent Catholicism'. This was opposed by those concerned for conciliation or moderation and who sought a rallying, a reassurance; they comprised a variety of different schools regrouped under the label 'liberal Catholicism'.

This simplified sketch is far from satisfactory, even if after two centuries the division constantly reappears, keeping alive among Catholics a never-ending dispute over the great historical watershed of the advent of 'modern society' and 'modern freedoms' in the wake of the French Revolution, or, more generally, the immense shock (1775–1815) which swept Europe and the Americas and which therefore has sometimes been called the 'Atlantic revolution'.

This revolution did not spare the church, which was affected in two ways: it was robbed of its former position and put on the defensive. Instead of being privileged and authoritative, it now found itself obliged to react, in conscience and in doctrine: it became reactionary, in opposition to the party of movement and progress. Within, it became involved in a vast intellectual debate which tore it apart: the relationship between the reform of the old order and the affirmation of new principles, the 'modern errors' which Pius XI listed in his 1864 *Syllabus*.

Thus a 'legitimist' Catholicism bound together throne and altar, the political past and religious truth, the restoration of what was with the model of what should be: in France the representatives of this trend were called 'ultras'. At the other extreme a 'liberal' Catholicism, which was far from limiting itself to politics, was able to turn the page and accept a new order established *de facto*, without sacrificing either the rights of the church or the teaching of the faith. For these 'liberal' Catholics the dead had to be left to bury their dead, and the choice had to be for the love of one's time and one's country.

The clash between the two parties was head-on, and no discussion was possible. At least it was simple. If history is not reduced to this mutual exclusiveness, it is because both liberals and ultras held firm to a traditional Catholicism which was neither ultra nor liberal and which took its directions from Rome. The wars of religion between Catholics and Protestants had ended up in the principle *cujus regio, ejus religio*, which in Europe was to bring the triumph of regalism: the sovereign is the temporal head of the religion of the country, and in Catholic countries the authority of the pope is limited to the spiritual sphere. In France this led to the Gallican Declaration of the Clergy (1682). The Revolution was to have the paradoxical effect of killing off regalism and thus of encouraging the blossoming of papalism, from Gregory XVI to the present day

The papacy did not have happy memories of the eighteenth century, the age of the Enlightenment, or of the seventeenth century, the age of Absolutism. Neither Pius VI in his condemnation of the Civil Constitution of the Clergy (1791) nor Pius VII hailing democracy proved to be very nostalgic about the *Ancien Régime*. Pius IX, who was hostile to the Risorgimento, was always loved far more than his successor by the Italians. Appealed to by the ultras and by the liberals, the papacy did not seek to trace out a *via media* between them, but found itself faced with a formidable problem of discernment and application.

In short, the Holy See could agree to reforms which instituted the new order (the French Concordat of 1801 is a striking proof of this) while condemning the new principles which legitimated this order. The reforms were in the realm of the contingent: one could think them good and judge them inopportune or risky; one could think them bad and become resigned to them in the name of higher considerations. The condition was that they should not be taken for principles of transform themselves into matters of principle.

Around 1860 some liberals made the famous distinction between thesis and hypothesis: classical theologians judged it inopportune since the thesis is always abstract, and to suppose that it is perfectly realized somewhere on earth involves a 'hypothesis'. Historical Christianity has never been just a hypothesis: the thesis is the Christianity of theology, i.e. a political theology based on the distinction and articulation of the 'two powers'. It was the basis of this theology which was undermined by the 'modern ideas' emerging from Lutheranism and the secularization which stemmed from them. So the great dispute over modernity has unfolded on three distinct but indissociable levels.

1. *A conflict within Catholicism*. Despite appearances, even in its sharpest phases, even in the confusions and waverings born of polemic, the opposition has never been a dichotomy between those who accept and those who reject 'modernity', that abstract word until recently (three or four decades ago) alien to Catholic vocabulary. It is a work of discernment through which a matter of conscience is resolved between ultras, intransigents and liberals. It is the contradictory interpretation of a historical situation, of what is at stake in it both theoretically and substantively. It is both casuistic and hermeneutic, associated with a mentality but never reduced to an intemporal ideality.

What is at stake here, whether noble or down-to-earth, is of the essence of this opposition: here is the real arena of the debate, which is never purely repetitive but at each stage takes in the facts of the situation. These two centuries of history are full of jousts like that which saw Las Casas and Sepulveda opposed in the sixteenth century. Both faced in the name of the demands of their faith what they thought to be an unprecedented situation. The delicate and necessary task of the historian here is to follow through time the shifts in the controversy of which those involved are rarely aware – as an analogy one might choose the adventures of Thomism over several centuries which claimed to have 'the mind of St Thomas' and then under the leadership of Leo XIII, who made it the framework of the *ordo rerum futurus* in the Catholic social spirit.

2. *The conflictual translation of this discernment into action*. Thomas Jefferson, who framed the principles to which the American Declaration of Independence of 1776 went back, would always recall – to his French friends in particular – the immense gap between theory and reality. He kept telling them that even in the United States, which enjoyed every favourable circumstance, it had not proved possible to apply in their entirety either the principles of the Declaration or the articles of the Constitution. 'Government of the people by the people' was no more than a polar star by which one could set a course; it was not a prefabricated plan. In its own way, through its divisive certainties and uncertainties, the Catholic Church has to live out this tension between a faith which all claim to share, an ideal of historical action in several versions, and a personal appreciation of the needs or opportunities of the moment.

3. *The presence of an alien body, an enemy outside*. This whole practice of Catholic reflection and action does not take place in an aseptic void, but in a hostile environment which adds its specific pressure to the course of the debates. Right-wing anti-clericalism and left-wing anti-clericalism (which can go as far as atheism) are matched on the Catholic side by an

anti-liberalism coupled with an anti-socialism, i.e. a twofold rejection. Whether in the form of Catholicism, liberalism or socialism, not to mention anarchism, intransigence is then the main thing to be shared, a characteristic common to all, whether in social relations or, even more, in ideas professed.

The problem is that it is difficult to isolate 'modernity' as an entity and to reduce everything to it. One always has to return to the different levels of everyday life. And confronted with an offensive, whether open or hidden, Catholics close ranks behind the pope, not sufficiently closely for some, too closely for others, in such a way that their reaction justifies a reinforcing of the hostility towards them.

Vague debates abound, for example around freedom of conscience and the Inquisition. Mistrust leads to rumour and fantasy. An amazing literature proliferates which sees suspicion and plotting everywhere. Some countries of Europe and Latin America are undergoing a real *Kulturkampf*. Those who are trying to come to an arrangement which is fair to both sides and who think it important to learn to live together in a society divided by convictions, find themselves caught up in a double excommunication.

It is almost impossible to trace a line from the ultras to the integralists, as one can from the liberals to the progressives. Rather, there is an ongoing situation in which the same patterns are reproduced in new circumstances. At all events, the debate is not Hamletian, 'to be or not to be' of one's time. Each person is of his or her time, but there are many ways of being in a society which does not follow universal time but often its own clock. Otherwise it would be necessary to write off all those who are not willing to go along, the last peasants who desperately resist agricultural policy, or the workers who are not needed by industrial restructuring. Here Péguy's sarcastic remark soon becomes relevant: 'They praise in the name of modernity what they condemn in the name of capitalism.' As a Catholic one cannot celebrate secularization and deplore its bulldozing effects, which lead to the alienation of the young from religion and the collapse of religious culture. The division among Catholics is the result of this situation, for which none of the three great currents has been able to find a remedy, a situation with which they could not have coped any better even had they achieved that union which has been so regularly desired. The hopes of Catholics, which were great and tenacious, have always been disappointed. Their failures, which have been numerous and severe, have always surprised them. Among them the roots of anti-modernity run deep and far even now, and not without strong reasons, whose nature is to be in no way sufficient.

Christians have no reason to despair as long as they do not confuse the virtue of hope with the forms given to their hopes: of reconquering the world, making Christians our brothers again, instituting a new Christianity or prophesying catastrophe; or, more recently, of inculturating faith in the world of this age, giving meaning to a human activity which is deprived of meaning. They have neither to condemn nor to rally 'modernity' but, in its crucible, to undergo the radical test that it imposes on them, a test unprecedented in human history.

Most Christians are at ease today and, while remaining critical, can profit from modernity without producing it. They are *acculturated* without having succeeded in the *inculturation* of which they so readily speak. They serve modernity: they do not direct it or influence its course. For half a century there have been enough Christians occupying key positions in politics and the economy for no one to have any illusions here.

The major axis of a contemporary history of the church should not be the exaltation of *efforts* made by Catholics – though these should not be underestimated or denied, whatever their orientation – but an examination of the obstacles that they have encountered. The history of Catholic anti-modernity is the equivalent of the history of Catholic anti-Modernism, a dimension which has not yet found its place in any of the scholarly histories of religion that we have.

For better or worse, 'modernity' has transformed our everyday life and our cultural horizon: how can we remain unaffected by it? How can we not admire this prodigious deployment of human genius? But surely we also have to ask about the cost, the promises broken, the illusions. Many people today *no longer believe*: they call themselves, or are called, 'post-moderns'. But these post-moderns are also post-Christians. The difficulty gets one degree worse. There is no question of a 'return'. The belief in a return of the religious after its eclipse rests on an ignorance of history: if the nineteenth century and even the beginning of the twentieth century were moderately Catholic, not to say Christian, they were powerfully religious.[1] Modernity has not ceased to produce the religious and its negation, which was itself sometimes very religious, while the modern activism of Catholics contributed to the 'de-Christianization' that they thought they were combatting. This is a major paradox of our time.

In short, modernity is what followed Catholicity, and each has its horizon of universality. Modernity has been and continues to be an immense revolution which has not been achieved in a day. Its progress has accelerated under our very eyes, without too much concern about where it is leading us. For a long time Christians and socialists have agreed in not counting their future dear. This is in fact the only revolution which has succeeded, imposing its law on the whole world. All dream of it and submit themselves to it. It has become our impassable horizon. A sociology of modernity must not limit itself to its values, its contradictions, its theme: it must be a sociology of a conquering dynamism which to this day is still unconquered, which has assimilated or brushed aside all criticisms, even the most profound. No criticism, no failure, no impasse has ever stopped it.

For the Roman Church, which has never had a monopoly of anti-modernity, the need was to survive in the face of an upheaval which caught it unawares and whose magnitude, consequences and power it was unable to measure. For a long time its great resource was resistance to what it saw as 'repudiation and apostasy', but it did not engage in any coherent or specific reflection. The church had a traditional teaching based on the principle of Catholicity: what value did that have in a modern world in which words were changing meaning, in which theological discourse no longer seemed open to the demands of the modern spirit or what was called the scientific approach?

Whether a displacement or a mutation, this discourse has been profoundly transformed but has not succeeded in establishing itself: its new versions fit no better, though they allow those who relate use it to follow the movement. Here we have what, strictly speaking, should be called 'Catholic modernism', instead of always being reduced to a local crisis, narrowly circumscribed and happily stamped out by the vigour of a holy pope. To measure the course covered is one of the conditions of judging what remains to be done.

We must not schematize or caricature the past that has elapsed nor the present with its difficulties. Is it too trivial to recall that at the beginning of modernity there was a revolution of the subject, an emergence of the conscience – prepared long before by centuries of Christianity – an affirmation of human autonomy, the triumph of the private sense? Is it too trivial to recall that the great novelty in human history over the past two centuries has not been what has been improperly called 'freedom of conscience' – Fénelon was already celebrating 'the impenetrable retrenchment of the freedom of the heart' without being contradicted – but public freedom of conscience for everyone without exception? But then must we not inevitably note the two corollaries: the status of truth and the criterion of objectivity, the governability of societies and the problem of power? The liberal revolution could be fought against as a 'crime of *lèse-vérité* and *lèse-société*'.[2] This was not a petty quarrel, nor a minor one.

We should never forget that Catholic anti-modernism lies at the source of the Catholic social movement of which Catholic Action has been the heart: a force for progress which has played a major role in history, but which does not fit in easily as a fruit of the Enlightenment and modernity. The conscience has remained the apple of discord between liberals and

Catholics. All that the latter are ready to accord it seems notoriously inadequate to the former. Are Christians ready to admit, in the name of modernity, that the conscience is sovereign, autonomous and creative in the last instance, that it has an authority of its own, a legislative authority? *Dictamen conscientiae* or *lex conscientiae*? That is the question discreetly evaded by too many debates on this subject. The *non possumus* is rooted in an intransigence which still has many happy days ahead, and can also make a good case for itself. The risk is that it will reduce itself to a stubborn excuse.

Translated by John Bowden

Notes

1. See my *Critique et mystique*, Paris 1984, ch. VII, 'Nouveaux christianismes et religion de l'humanité'.
2. Auguste Nicolas, *L'état sans Dieu, Mal Social de France*, Paris 1872, 84; 'Un déicide social', 22.

The Philosophical Critique of Modernity

Helmut Peukert

I. The crisis of modernity and philosophical reflection

At present there seems to be a growing impression that we are at a threshold in history at which previous interpretations and orientations are becoming questionable and new ones must be sought. Historically, the contours of a historical period are emerging, and the basic tendencies which determined it are becoming clear. So there is justification for speaking of modernity as an era, even if its beginnings can be traced back to the thirteenth and fourteenth centuries, and in its full manifestation in the last two and a half centuries it merely represents the front of a human cultural development which is generally accelerating.

What makes us speak of the critical threshold of an era is the impression that the effects of modernity as a social development which in terms of its dynamics is constantly overtaking itself are rebounding on it and endangering it. As a historical movement modernization is objective and reflex, in that it threatens itself. That calls for criticism, reflection and the search for alternative ways of dealing with reality, including philosophy.

In this article I want first to attempt to describe the tendencies of the development of modern societies, and then to try to explain against this background above all the analyses of the criticial theory of the 'Frankfurt School' and the reflections of more recent French philosophy which tend to be summed up under different names like anti-humanism, post-structuralism or post-modern. In conclusion I shall indicate the questions which seem to me to remain open here – for theology as well.

II. The development of modern societies

What are the phenomena which allow us to mark out modernity as an era and also take into account its basic tendencies in philosophy? There are probably above all three innovations which at the same time lead to an inner differentiation of modern societies into sub-systems. For the sphere of culture in the modern sense there are the modern sciences, for the economic sphere there is the capitalist market economy, and for the sphere of politics the democratic state.

People are most likely to accept the thesis that the rise of modern science marks an epoch-making break. What is decisively new is procedure by which another understanding of reality is outlined hypothetically. This is then used to test experiences which are themselves in turn only gained from experiments outlined in the light of the hypotheses. The transition to increasing knowledge through trial and error, carried through systematically, presupposes an attitude that everything could be different from what it has appeared to be so far and now appears, and that error no longer receives social sanction. The mutability of a contingent reality is matched by the increased power of control of the subject, which is itself contingent and attempts to assert itself by increasing its knowledge.

The second fundamental change relates to attitudes to trade and the economy. Recent historical investigations have shown how long it took for Adam Smith's thesis that pursuing one's own material interests furthered the common good to establish itself, through controversy and in the face of abiding doubt. It was this thesis which gave moral legitimation to the capitalist market economy and the expression of economic rationality as the calculation of individual advantage in conditions of scarcity. When Bernard de Mandeville presented this theory for the first time in 1714 in his fable of the bees, in England he could still be castigated as the 'man devil'.

The interplay of the capitalist market economy and modern science released a dynamic the consequences of which there was no obvious means of bringing under control. Thomas Hobbes posed in an acute way the problem how a society in which everyone is the rival, indeed the enemy of another, can survive. For him it seemed possible to control the mechanism of the competitive struggle if everyone agreed, purely out of an interest in survival, to create a central state authority equipped with the authority to keep individuals from mutual annihilation. It subsequently became clear that this authority becomes a totalitarian dictatorship unless insight into the limits of the rationality at its disposal leads to the discovery of a system of dividing up authority, of checks and balances, which limit both the claims of centralized power and also the damage done by the competitive struggle of individuals. The question then is whether modern societies can control the dynamic which they themselves have unleashed with the form of democratic constitutions that they have given themselves so far.

At present there is an impression that the consequences of the intensifying tendencies in the individual dimensions of human action, which are mutually fortifying one another, can no longer be diverted externally or internally, but rebound on us from the limits of a finite system. It is to be feared that our action will thus become self-destructive in a paradoxical way. The economic system which is meant to secure the satisfaction of basic needs is endangering the very foundations of our life. The political and administrative system which is meant to ensure peaceful coexistence can no longer control the mechanisms of increasing power and can only answer threats of annihilation with threats which can result in self-annihilation. The socio-cultural system which is to enable more self-determination through an extension of communication is threatening to produce greater isolation, and under the influence of an international media industry to lead to fragmented and fictionalized consciousness. And all this is taking place all over the world, and is having an increasingly sharp effect on the growing populations of the so-called underdeveloped countries which are more directly vulnerable to these mechanisms than the lands of the North, and more than they must destroy the basis of the life of future generations to secure present survival.

It is in this basic situation that the consequences of tendencies in the development of modern societies are beginning to emerge and call for an extreme effort, if they are to be understood theoretically and finally overcome in practical terms. Here it seems worthwhile to describe the efforts which have been undertaken by the Frankfurt School with its critical theory and by contemporary French philosophers.

III. Modernity among the classic figures of the Frankfurt School

Historians and interpreters have shown that it is impossible to explain the unitary theory which has united the various creative thinkers from such different disciplines as economics, psychology, literary and cultural theory, and social philosophy who from 1931 gathered around Max Horkheimer and his Institute of Social Research in Frankfurt. But there were experiences which disturbed all the representatives of these disciplines, and these included both the rise of authoritarian movements and finally Fascist systems in Southern and Central Europe, and the degeneration of the Russian Revolution into Stalinism. If one wanted to explain these developments, then obviously neither Marx's theory of the development of capitalist societies nor Max Weber's theory of the origin of modern societies from processes of rationalization and administrative-bureaucratic power would be enough. If we wish to speak of a hard core to the research programme of critical theory in its first phase, it lay in an approach in terms of social psychology, which combined Marx's theory of society with Freud's psychoanalysis and was above all meant to explain how authoritarian social structures could come into being rather than relations of solidarity, and how they are reproduced and anchored psychologically.

So the methodology of this research programme was very much in the tradition of that 'hermeneutic of suspicion' of which Paul Ricoeur spoke later. For it, even one's own consciousness was no longer an absolute. Rather, Cartesian doubt was now turned against consciousness, and the social and individual mechanisms of its constitution were discovered. This was meant to lead to a comprehensive concept of consciousness and reason, and the concept of a transformatory practice which made it possible to break through social and psychological mechanisms and realize this reason.

However, under the impact of the Second World War and the Holocaust which was beginning, this programme lost its power of conviction. In the light of these limit experiences, what in Western history had been called reason or Enlightenment came under the suspicion of being only the will to self-assertion and control, which must finally become the will to annihilate others and oneself. This line was developed by the *Dialectic of Enlightenment*[1] which M. Horkheimer and T. W. Adorno had written in 1943/44, at the height of the industrialized annihilation of people on battlefields and in concentration camps. For Horkheimer and Adorno, human beings as rational beings are part of nature. However, reason is at the same time the capacity to detach oneself from the context of nature, to take one's distance from it, to become autonomous and assert oneself. This capacity for distancing contains the possibility of transforming nature into the object of domination. The concept which identifies the particular as a universal can also lead to this transformation.[2] The abstraction of the resistance of the particular and its identification as a universal is a preparation for manipulation. This is intensified by mathematically formalized theory. Theory becomes the means of dominating reality and increasing power. The motive for this domination is ultimately the anxiety of being dominated oneself, because rivals can similarly increase their power. Thus the will to self-assertion as a will to dominate nature necessarily becomes the will to dominate other people. But this form of self-assertion can succeed only if people also dominate themselves in order to increase their possibilities for action. Human beings dominate themselves in order to dominate others, so as not to be dominated themselves.

Thus for Horkheimer and Adorno reason becomes self-contradictory. On the one hand it contains the idea of a free human society. At the same time, however, it forms the authority of calculating thought which damages the world for the purposes of self-preservation. This is the perspective in which Auschwitz could appear as the endpoint of a disastrous development of European and human culture generally: the subsumption of things and people under formal identifying concepts which in the process exclude the refractory non-identical; the social establishment of rival systems for intensifying domination in economics and politics, which utilize everything for purposes of self-assertion, including a science reduced to instrumental rationality, and finally the transformation of people into material – and in all this the perversion of reason so that it becomes an instrument of domination.

Under the influence of extreme limit experiences the theoreticians of critical theory increasingly went back to Jewish theological traditions. Walter Benjamin was their main advocate. In conversations and arguments with Adorno and Horkheimer it was accepted as unthinkable that current theological language could continue to be used. Here they went too far in fusing the Old Testament prohibition of images with radical criticism of any objectifying metaphysics, but the motive of historical materialism was also too strong for the historical process to be looked at from the perspective of its victims. Rather, it was thought necessary to maintain the historical negativity and insist on a 'radicalization of dialectic to its glowing theological nucleus'.[3]

For Walter Benjamin, remembering the dead, the 'revolutionary tiger's leap into the past',[4] shatters the continuity of a period of time which is thought of as a history of progress. The moment of remembering releases the intimation of another configuration. There cannot be universal solidarity, in other words a proleptic solidarity with future generations, without anamnetic solidarity. The idea of a linear history of progress is to be destroyed, not only because the linear progress rebounds on itself and threatens itself, but because the intrinsic contradictoriness of a linear conception of history has become clear. New concepts of time, intersubjectivity and solidarity in its historical dimension are to be developed from the experience of the slaughtered victims. Only then can it become clear what human action could mean in a catastrophic history.

One cannot claim that the representatives of the first generation of critical theory had a conception which was worked out in all dimensions. But they had identified a problem which neither philosophical nor theological reflection may fall short of.

IV. The dialectic of modernity and post-modernity in French anti-humanism

The experience of a modernization which is a threat to itself also determines the directions of philosophical thought which can be described as post-modern, post-structuralist or anti-humanist. The multiplicity of designations shows that this is not a unitary direction and that this thought is taken up and developed in very different ways. The post-modern perspective attempts to look at an era as a unity of the principles which structure it. Thus post-modernity cannot be understood without the preceding structuralism in ethnology, linguistics and psychoanalysis. But it also seeks to distinguish itself from a thought which had made an anonymous, unconscious, overarching system of rules directing conscious life itself a determining factor.

Here thinkers like Derrida or Lyotard resolutely go back to Nietzsche and Heidegger. Heidegger[5] had attempted to reconstruct the history of Western thought generally as the history of an increasingly radical way of dealing with reality in the form of power. The proximity of at least these theses to some of the views of classical critical theory has often been noted. To put it extremely briefly, Heidegger sees as the basic feature of Western thought the fact that man as subject understands all entities as object in such a way that these can only fall within the horizon of a notional scheme and thus become and remain open to calculation and manipulation. This subject is itself dominated by the will to secure its subjectness. It is will for itself, and as such will for power. The will for power is intrinsically concerned to intensify itself. It wants itself to be a will which intensifies its power – and no more than that. The history of Western thought, of Western 'metaphysics', is thus increasingly radical nihilism.

That explains how French anti-humanism can proclaim the 'death of man' after the death of God and understand itself as protest against a 'humanistic' tradition which can think of people only as subjects of domination. Anti-humanism seeks to be a more radical humanism and to conceive of a more radical form of humanity. The connection here with Nietzsche is plain. In elemental productivity, Zarathustra's 'Superman', who has left the 'last men' behind him, breaks through all forms of thought and conduct aimed at purely securing his own existence and recreates himself as a freedom which posits itself. The will for creative freedom seeks to gain itself in new immediacy and innocence and to create a more original morality.

For Derrida as for Lyotard, Nietzsche's and Heidegger's thought, like that of Foucault, opens up the possibility of perceiving the crisis of reason which is the result of the history of the West and beginning to overcome it. Here Lyotard[6] refers to the results of epistemological and mathematical-logical research like Gödel's theorem of indeterminability or Wittgenstein's thesis of the plurality of incommensurable language games which cannot be reduced to each other, in order to develop a concept of language which does not allow any unity without contradiction. Conflict, 'le différend', is omnipresent.[7] Derrida[8] is concerned to overcome a way of thinking which constructs a unity, a basis to provide security, a centre as presence which can be understood and ultimately controlled. The important thing is not to construct a unity and subject oneself to it; it is the irreducible 'différance' through which differences are established and presence is pushed aside (différer). This is meant to make possible another form of temporality, another form of dealing with oneself, with others and with reality generally.

What are we to make of this thought? Closer analysis would have to discuss the roots of French post-modernism also in Jewish thought, in the tradition of Talmudic interpretation. Generally speaking, however, we must ask whether thought in terms of difference really preserves the otherness of the other or whether the play of differences does not ultimately lead to indifference towards others and to the conjuring up of an indeterminate authority. These, at any rate, are the questions which Jürgen Habermas raises, and his thought allows us to clarify some problems of the discussion so far.

V. The project of modernity in the thought of Jürgen Habermas

While in content Habermas's thought must be understood as a continuation of the work of the first generation of critical theorists, it differs from their conception. In his view the older critical theory could understand modern rationality only as technical and instrumental, and the active subject only as a subject of domination. It is important to Habermas from the start to explicate a form of action in which the other is recognized as a partner with equal rights. So he was concerned to develop a theory of intersubjective action which is free of domination and which could serve as a basis both for a theory of the subject and for intersubjectivity, and for a critical theory of society. Thus his starting point is not the monological subject acting intentionally, but subjects which from the start are bound together in a world which they have in common, which has been produced through history and is interpreted by language.[9] However, for Habermas this starting point from a subject which is as it were 'decentred' from the beginning does not necessarily lead to the dissolution of the subject or to its violent self-assertion through domination; rather, it proves to be a normative basic structure of the capacity to speak which I recognize in the act of speaking, the acknowledgment of a conversation partner who can respond to me. To acknowledge that the other is different and has equal status to me is the norm which is always already presumed and at the same time the goal and thus also the criterion of the critique of communication.[10]

Against this background Habermas attempts to clarify the development of individuals and societies in their interdependence and to discover foundations for the pathologies of both. He attempts this through a reconstruction of social differentiation by stages which makes it clear how sub-systems of purposive rational action are gradually separated off from a world orientated on communication, how they extend and overlay and consume elements of tradition which have grown up. The threshold of modernity in particular is marked out by that process of rationalization by an instrumental and functionalist 'reason' which 'colonializes' the world and its communicative reason. For Habermas, the pathologies of modern societies can be explained in terms of the dominant power of the economic system on the one hand and the political-administrative system on the other, each with its functional pressures which extend into spheres which, by their constitution, depend on the priority of unforced communicative action. Pathological developments of the individual can then also be explained as a transplanting of the pathologies of society.

In this way different basic categories are developed for a theory of modernity. The power and force of functional systems is contrasted with a potential of communicative reason which has a history by genre and individual that has expressed itself historically not only in post-conventional ethics but also in modern legal systems and constitutions. It is a potential which allows the continuation of the project of modernity as the project of an Enlightenment which is enlightening about itself.

In the critical argument between Habermas and French representatives of post-modernity[11] it has emerged that each side has difficulty in understanding the other: this problem evidently arises from differences of cultural and political background. The criticism of a rationalism established institutionally which knows only itself as a criterion inevitably makes a different impact in the French cultural sphere from that in a land which has got to know the suppression of any public rational argumentation in a Fascist system. But even if one attempts to reconstruct the different fronts of the critical discussion of modernity, a number of fundamental unsolved problems remain.

VI. Open questions

(a) The reconstruction of an epoch like modernity in philosophical terms threatens to level out its internal differences. Lyotard's talk of the 'great stories' ('*grands récits*') of the Enlightenment and liberation tends to suppress their inner contradictions. The 'hermeneutic of difference' is in danger of thinking only of the other of one's own thought instead of perceiving the other thought of others. However, the history of the Enlightenment is a history of radical reflection on oneself, not only a history of the self-destructive 'dialectic of enlightenment' but also a history of the self-enlightening effect of the Enlightenment. If one excludes the critical alternatives, one deprives oneself of irreplacable historical potential. And what alternative could there be to a self-critical Enlightenment?

(b) 'Anti-humanism' protests against the reduction of man to a manipulating subject of domination which levels down all individual differences, and calls for the recognition of otherness. But often this means only the recognition of another in one's own self, another to reason, consciousness, language. The recognition of the otherness of the concrete other person falls into the background. Emmanuel Lévinas has therefore insisted on the 'humanism of the other person'.[12] For him, an ethics of the recognition of the otherness of other people is the 'first philosophy', from which a definition of language, consciousness and reason has to start. The central philosophical question is then: how can a communication be conceived which concedes and acknowledges the inalienable individuality of the other precisely in the process of understanding?

(c) Philosophers do not live in a sphere apart from society. Their thought is taken up not only in the sciences but also in public discussion and thus in the media, and often serves to legitimate social developments. Even if it may go against the intention of its authors, often unclear talk of 'difference' seems to meet up with two particular tendencies of social development. First, the increase in the complexity of modern society leads to an increased individualization, indeed atomization, of individuals. Secondly, all cultural achievements, even those of avant-garde art, are integrated with increasing rapidity into the economic process of evaluation of a media industry which is linked together internationally, and this contributes to the increasing fictionalization and fragmentation of the world of everyday life and robs it of its communicative substructure. But the central cultural task after the dissolution of traditional structures should consist specifically in building up a communicative world at a new level of consciousness.

(d) That is true not only of the world of everyday life but also of the public, political sphere. In their development, modern societies have meanwhile come to be a threat to themselves. If this is not to lead to escapism from the situation or to authoritarian or even totalitarian reactions, new organs are needed for social self-perception and for arriving at common decisions. This calls for far-reaching processes of learning, both individual and collective.[13] For all the tendencies towards 'deconstruction', a philosphical theory of modernity faces the task of collaborating constructively in the development of a new form of democratic 'constitution' in which scientific, political and moral learning-processes are interconnected, and given a lasting form which can continually be put to the test. Such a 'reflective constitutionalism' orientated on transforming praxis could also be a new place for dialogue between philosophy, social theory and theology.

Translated by John Bowden

Notes

1. M. Horkheimer and T.W. Adorno, *Dialectic of Enlightenment*, New York and London 1975.
2. T.W. Adorno, *Negative Dialectics*, New York and London 1973.
3. Letter, 'Adorno to Benjamin', 2 August 1935, in T.W. Adorno, *Über Walter Benjamin*, ed. R. Tiedeman, Frankfurt 1975, 117.
4. W. Benjamin, 'Theses on the Philosophy of History', in *Illuminations*, London 1973.
5. M. Heidegger, 'Überwindung der Metaphysik', in *Vorträge und Aufsätze*, Pfullingen 1954.
6. J.-F. Lyotard, *Das postmoderne Wissen*, Paris 1979.
7. J.-F. Lyotard, *Le différend*, Paris 1983.
8. J. Derrida, 'Die différance', in P. Englemann (ed.), *Postmoderne und Dekonstruktion. Texte französischer Philosophen der Gegenwart*, Stuttgart 1990; Derrida, *L'écriture et la différence*, Paris 1967.
9. J. Hamermas, *The Theory of Communicative Action* (2 vols), London and Boston 1987.
10. H. Peukert, *Science, Action, and Fundamental Theology: Towards a Theology of Communicative Action*, Cambridge, Mass. 1984.
11. J. Habermas, *The Philosophical Discourse of Modernity: Twelve Lectures*, Cambridge, Mass. 1987.
12. E. Levinas, *L'humanism de l'autre homme*, Paris 1973.
13. H. Peukert, *Bildung und Vernunft*, Frankfurt (forthcoming).

Attempts at Reconciling Modernity and Religion in Catholic and Protestant Theology

Christoph Theobald

Any attempt to identify in the theology of the nineteenth and twentieth centuries a shared concern to reconcile religion (in this case Christian religion) and modernity today comes up against a twofold difficulty.

First, a purely emblematic, not to say mythical, use of the concept of modernity runs the risk of disguising the complexity of the historical process envisaged by this term. There are in fact several modernities, and this process of differentiating cultural spheres and their respective rationalities, in brief the slow exodus of European civilization from a holistic universe, is manifested in theology primarily as a diversification of disciplines, so characteristic of theological faculties since the nineteenth century. Some theologians have opposed scientific modernity, which from the seventeenth century in successive waves has introduced a new relationship between human beings and nature: they have tried to reformulate their faith in connection with one scientific cosmology or another. Others have tended, rather, to enter into discussion with political modernity, which is inseparable from an economic and social modernity, and which from the end of the eighteenth century has transformed human relations; they have developed a moral theology or a political and social ethic which has largely contributed to redefining relations between churches, societies and states. Yet others have taken the ground of cultural modernity, which since the beginning of this century has secularized relations between individual and religious institutions, relativizing them in relation to other social bonds: they are inspired by the new philosophy of religion, integrating it into a fundamental theology which associates Christian believing with the basic value of freedom of conscience.

Much rarer are those who, in this increasingly specialized university context, have arrived at an overall view, a theology of their own, coming to grips with a differentiated rationality, free both from the holism of their churches and the pietisms of all kinds which thought that they could resolve the conflict with modernity by protecting faith from all rationality.

A second difficulty arises at this point, by virtue of the fact that the concept of modernity does not denote just a historical process of cultural and rational differentiation but also a value judgment which transforms progress into a cultural imperative (Baudrillard). Modernity necessarily implies a conflict in the interpretation of itself. Now to speak of a reconciliation between religion and modernity suggests a direct encounter between two well-defined entities, not to say between two hostile sisters: as if modernity were at root anti- or areligious and religion essentially anti-modern. This judgment, which was certainly largely shared in the eighteenth and nineteenth centuries, derives from myth and forgets that the partners in the debate have their places in the same history of differentiation and secularization, in orientation at the mercy of their interpretations. The theologians on whom I would want to reflect in this article have been able to move, often before their respective churches and sometimes in conflict with them, from the myth of modernity to a true historical awareness which submits both the history of modern times and the religious phenomenon to an act of interpretation.

In this adventure, Protestant and Catholic theology did not start from the same point, nor did they meet with the same resistance, nor did they have the same resources. So we must first of all try to understand why these two traditions are out of phase.

A proverbial difference in phase

In the nineteenth century, a good deal of Protestantism in fact identified itself with the cause of a scientific modernity. One might recall the remark by Paul Tillich, making not without pride a survey of two hundred years of historical-critical research in the biblical field: 'It appears that no other religion in human history exercised such boldness and took upon itself the same risk. Certainly Islam, orthodox Judaism and Roman Catholicism did not do so.'[1]

However, at the beginning of the Enlightenment in the eighteenth century, Protestant theology found itself up against significant resistance. In its doctrine of verbal inspiration 'Lutheran orthodoxy' had identified the letter of the Bible with the word of God. The practice of criticism thus brought about a real revolution which drew the Word itself into the secular sphere of historical relativity, posing the hermeneutical question of meaning in a totally unprecedented way. The importance of this fundamental decision, which recurs in all the 'theologies of reconciliation' within Protestantism, cannot be emphasized enough. It reverses the basic orientation of the Reformation, which went from the Word towards faith, substituting for this the anthropocentric logic of an autonomous quest for meaning. Certainly, since Semler (1725–1791), attempts have been made to re-root historical-critical practice in the Lutheran doctrine of justification which, according to Ebeling, 'delivers faith over totally to the tribulations and ambiguities of history' (1950). But it is easy to see how this formulation is an anthropological reinterpretation of the Reformation *sola fide* in terms of a completely new historical practice.

However, one cannot disqualify all these re-readings of the Lutheran tradition from the start as simple adaptations to the spirit of the Enlightenment. The greatest figures, like Lessing, Herder, Kant or Schleiermacher, were well able to ask questions, and critical ones too, about the relevance of the historical-critical method both for religion and for Christian faith. Perhaps there was a risk that their historical awareness, which had barely emerged, would be swallowed up in a progressivist or emancipatory vision of the history of humanity, in their view governed by a slow divine education towards the universalism of reason, a universalism which was perfectly compatible with a spiritual and moral practice of the 'eternal gospel'. In fact their attempts at reconciliation are based on the theological presupposition that Christianity is above all a faith in God, living and new at each moment, and that the justification of the sinner is not a work of Christ but a direct operation of God, inherent in the act of faith. So this operation can only impose itself through its own moral force, leaving to historical facts (the work of Christ and the church) merely a role of illustration, and never of demonstration.

Without too much artificiality one can distinguish between three phases in the development of these theologies of reconciliation. Their prehistory ends with Schleiermacher, who set the tone for the whole of the nineteenth century. With him the concept of religion acquires its own status, independent of any metaphysical and moral reduction, centred on the 'intuition of the universe' and 'sentiment' (not to be confused with sentimental subjectivism). By reason of its infinite character, the religious phenomenon issues in a necessary and insurmountable plurality of historical expressions which from now on come under a general hermeneutic carried on by the faculty of philosophy, which thus becomes the real intellectual centre of the university. However, Schleiermacher describes Christianity as a 'religion of religion' and continues in his *Christian Faith* to give a mediating function for Christian faith to the religious personality of Christ, to his evocative power, acting through the community and through the expressiveness of the images of the gospel.

It is on this point that most of his successors begin to part company with him, describing his reconciliation as a 'mixed form' (to use Troeltsch's term). D.F-Strauss, the Tübingen school and several major historians like J. Wellhausen, A. Kuenen and A. von Harnack then set in place what one can call the 'liberal paradigm'. This brings about a divorce between the person of Jesus and the idea of the Christian faith. Historical criticism, thinking in the name of a scientific centrality that it can reconstruct the past in all its objectiveness, no longer leaves any doubt about the impossibility of surmounting the difference between the historical Jesus and the Christ of the primitive community. The former appears as the incomparable successor to the prophets, a man perfectly free where tradition is concerned, a patient master who separates religion from politics and the cult and preaches the way of inner peace with oneself and with God. If we have to stop following primitive Christianity in seeing him as the unsurpassable redeemer, history does authorize us to understand him as the starting point for the Christian world and to give his image a symbolic and pedagogical value.

With the suppression of the idea of the redeemer Christ, liberal theology equally did away with any form of ecclesiastical and cultic community. We might recall Wellhausen's remarks that 'the nation is more certainly God's creation than the church, and God more certainly works in the history of the nations than in that of the church'.[2] From now on the nation state and its political rationality become the real sphere where the religion of the modern individual can unfold.

The power of this liberal paradigm cannot be overestimated. Its structure has been maintained, even when the assurance of its underlying rationality has been somewhat shaken. It has proved possible to speak of its resurgence in Bultmannian theology, and it still serves as a main point of reference in dividing the history of Protestant theology into periods. It has not been superseded by those who, like Barth after the First World War, challenged any attempt at reconciliation between modernity and Christian faith. The shifts were produced by Ernst Troeltsch and others who, in the name of their historical practice, could not remain insensitive to the difference between the ideal of humanity in liberal theology and a Jesus who was immersed in a very different vision of the world, and who did not want, either, to renounce the communitarian and cultic aspect of Christianity in the name of their knowledge of the social history of religions. At the beginning of this century they inaugurated a third phase in the theological project of a reconciliation with modernity, to which we shall return at the end.

Up until the end of the nineteenth century, Catholicism lagged well behind this Protestant adventure. But more than that needs to be said. The theological resistance here was of quite a different order. The identification between the Word and Scripture in Lutheran orthodoxy was matched in post-Tridentine Catholicism by a confusion between the gospel and dogma. But what was of no consequence for a church of the spoken word, a baroque church characterized by emotion and decoration, remaining largely aloof from all modern criticism, became a major obstacle when a beginning was made, in a revolutionary context, to oppose the principles of dogma and authority with freedom of historical research. Paradoxically it was necessary to wait for the Thomistic renewal at the end of the nineteenth century for Catholic theology to rediscover in its own patrimony rational potentialities and a theology of redemption other than that of Augustine, which could be reconciled with the modern spirit.

The Catholic turning point

Certainly there were contacts with philosophies of history, as is indicated by the Catholic school of Tübingen, or Newman, but their ally was more the romanticism of Hammann, Herder or Schelling, himself at some points reacting against the liberal paradigm. The new impulse was to come once again (as with Schleiermacher) from the philosophy of religion.

At the end of the last century Maurice Blondel (1861–1949) in fact developed a new style of Catholic theology as it grappled with modernity, through his *Action* (1893) and his *Letter on Apologetic* (1896).[3] This style was to be followed as far as H. Bouillard, H. de Lubac and Karl Rahner (with Maréchal as an intermediary) and left profound traces in the texts of Vatican II.

According to Blondel, this reconciliation presupposes that one renounces none of the most specific demands of the Catholic conception of revelation or the legitimate rights of reason. It is in effect less such and such a dogma or such and such a gift of God which comes up against the demand of modern man for autonomy and his ideal of humanity as *the very form and fact of the gift*. Free in its source, it is none the less inevitable, imposed and obligatory for the humanization of the one for whom it is destined, in such a way that from a theological perspective there is no symmetry between the faith and a neutral or negative attitude, considered primarily as a failing or a wound in the person. 'If it is true that the demands of revelation are well founded, once cannot say that we are completely at home with ourselves; and there must be a trace of this inadequacy, this impotence, this demand in man *qua* man, and an echo in the most autonomous philosophy.'[4] Blondel then returns to philosophy, and to the philosophy of religion in particular, to decipher these traces of an openness of human beings, society and nature to transcendence, and a demonstration of the anthropological or transcendental base of the act of faith. According to Blondel, it is guaranteed that philosophy here does not go beyond its limits or sell off the most sacred rights of an autonomous reason by a purely formal approach to human action and its basic openness, an approach which is always incompetent when it is a matter of making a pronouncement on the effective reality of a transcendence and a divine communication addressed to human beings.

This methodological quest for traces, Blondel's 'method of immanence', in fact indicates a quite specific Catholic style. It can be identified in all the inductive or ascendant theologies of the twentieth century which try to open up 'access' to the Christian mystery from human, social, political and cultural realities, even if these attempts do not always attain the scientific and philosophical magnitude of Blondel's project. His basic intuition can be found again, for example, in Rahner's 1941 lectures on 'man hearing the Word' and in the preliminary exposition 'The Situation of Man in the World Today' of the Vatican II Constitution *Gaudium et Spes* of 1965, to give just two examples.

Unlike the Protestant attempts at reconciliation, this Catholic style is primarily based on a strictly dogmatic reflection. For Blondel (1896) and later for Rahner (1954), a re-reading of the dogma of Chalcedon opens up a field which allows the introduction of anthropology (as 'deficient christology') at the centre of theology. Blondel had already reflected in this framework on the theme of the incarnation, clearly opting for the Scotist thesis which 'envelops the mystery of the Man-God in the primitive plan of creation' instead of understanding it as the consequence 'of an original sin and with a view to a bloody redemption'.[5] Here redemption and justification are clearly put at the heart of the relationship between God and man, which makes it possible later (for example in Rahner's case) to take up the thorny question of the salvific causality of the death of Christ in Christian faith, a problem kept in suspense since historical criticism of the figure of the redeemer by liberal theology.

A second characteristic of this new theological style in effect lies in an interest in history, albeit extended to universal dimensions. From Blondel and Teilhard de Chardin to Rahner, attempts are made to rediscover the word of God 'which lightens every man' (John 1.9) and the traces of 'him in whom all subsists' (Col. 1.17) in the evolution and self-transcendent movement of the universe. The very history of humanity and in particular the advent of its autonomy in modern times is linked to the mystery of Christ as interpreted by Chalcedon, to the degree that the ever more intimate union between man and God does not signify a diminution of human creativity, but on the contrary increasingly reinforces it by a rigorous distinction between the two orders of nature and grace.

So one can understand that reference to the authority of St Thomas, constant since Leo XIII and often used in an anti-modernist sense, can change its significance in this christological framework. The work of the *'Doctor communis'* suddenly reveals an anthropocentric rationality little exploited hitherto, which allows the rediscovery (and recovery for Catholicsm) of the roots of modernity, beyond a Lutheran genealogy, in mediaeval Christianity. So one can also understand how the most disturbing results of historical criticism are more easily made harmless by a global interpretation of Christian faith which from the start knows itself to be in tune with the best inspirations of modernity.

Finally, and this is the third aspect of the Catholic theologies of reconciliation, this anthropological christocentrism will produce some shifts in ecclesiology. Certainly, the societal structure of the church and its hierarchical or dogmatic constitution will not be denied; but understanding the church essentially as an extension of the incarnation, theologians will put more stress on its anthropological basis, which is both individual and collective. To give just two examples: this change is expressed in a new interest in lay movements and the spiritual or even mystical character of the ecclesial body. Here one need only recall the impact of Fr Congar's works relating to the laity and Fr de Lubac's *Catholicism* (The Social Aspects of Dogma).

A theological modernity aware of its own limits

It is evident that attempts at reconciling modernity and religion do not get a good press today. They are often criticized in the name of what is sometimes called post-modernity, which would see in the Enlightenment a degree of totalitarianism of reason and the reconstruction of a religious neo-traditionalism on the basis of this criticism.

This criticism can find support, in fact, in two weighty arguments. Two world wars (for Protestant theology, above all the first), the subsequent problems of decolonization and the decay of the great ideologies at the present time have severely shaken the anthropocentrism of the Enlightenment and the ambition for a unification of the world around European rationality.

Besides, according to some, the apostolic project which underlay attempts at reconciliation notably in the Catholic sphere and in the great movements of Catholic Action has not kept its promises. One might think here of the famous speech supposed to be addressed by socialist Christians to their contemporaries and reported by Blondel in *The Bordeaux Social*

Week and Monophorism (1909),[6] which reflects on the logic of social experiences and the teachings which arise out of collective errors, ending up by this immanent way in 'the return of individuals and peoples to Christianity by some of the very ways that had first of all alienated them'. 'With you we seek', they say, 'positive solutions to the positive problems which the very development of scientific civilization constantly renews and complicates. But in the life of peoples and individuals there are hours of reflection and decisive choice. The latent work of truth in us comes sooner or later to the point where it has to make free use of its reason and its freedom, either to descend back below itself by an abuse of light and grace, imprisoning itself in the highest certainties and obligations, or to mount upwards to the complete truth of which the Catholic Church has the deposit.'[7] Can one truly say that this patient crossing of socio-political and cultural mediations has been crowned with the missionary success originally expected by the theological and pastoral approach to reconciliation with modernity?

The difference in phase between the Christian traditions I have mentioned perhaps explains why the Protestant reactions to these attempts at reconciliation already appear after the First World War, in dialectical theology, while in the Catholic sphere the same questions were not asked until the eve of Vatican II. From that time on, the theology of Hans Urs von Balthasar played a crystallizing role similar to that played by the theology of Karl Barth in the Protestant sphere. Other reactions, more political or more pietistic, will be presented elsewhere in this issue.

In conclusion, I would prefer to emphasize that the 'theologians of reconciliation' themselves, some from the beginning of this century and in line with the presuppositions of modernity, brought about a transformation of their theological rationality which anticipates the later criticisms of the myth of modernity, but without departing from its historical framework. In fact Ernst Troeltsch (1865–1923) inaugurated a third phase of the theological project of a reconciliation with modernity; in the Catholic sphere, these transformations are more marginal, and are manifested above all among the protagonists of the 'Modernist crisis' (1893–1913).

They have a common feature: an increasingly differentiated rationality, marked by the humanities of the time. Their historical awareness led them, particularly since the First World War, to ask questions over both about the future of modern societies and the future form of the Christian faith. These questions, very remote from the progressivism of the Enlightenment, manifest themselves in a growing sensitivity to cultural transformations and in an ever-extended awareness of the religious pluralism of humanity and the plurality of forms of socialization within the Christian tradition.

So do we not need from now on to understand Christian believing in a framework of a hermeneutical rationality which combines in a new way the strong points of each Christian confession, the reference to the gospel *and* experience in the church, which is both one and infinitely diverse. Probably we need even to rethink the identity of Christ and the Christian in the experience of believing and to show at what point the ultimate detachment which it inaugurates at the same time frees real cultural creativity at the level of biblical creativity.

These questions, which have haunted theology since the beginning of this century, call for interdisciplinary and essentially theological work, rooted in a church which has become more and more of a minority in our modern societies. Perhaps this work will have some chance of success if we remember that there is no 'reconciliation' without conversion.

Translated by John Bowden

Notes

1. Paul Tillich, *Systematic Theology* II, Chicago and London 1957, 107.
2. J. Wellhausen, 'Israel', *Encyclopaedia Britannica*⁹ 1879, reprinted as an appendix to his *Prolegamena to the History of Ancient Israel*, Cleveland 1957, 513.
3. Maurice Blondel, 'Lettre sur les exigences de la pensée contemporaine en matière d'apologétique et sur la methode de la philosophie dans l'étude du problème religieux', in *Les premiers écrits de Maurice Blondel*, Paris 1956.
4. Ibid., 37.
5. Ibid., 89.
6. M. Blondel, *La semaine sociale de Bordeaux et le monophorisme*, Paris 1910.
7. Ibid., 22f.

II · Postmodernity: Its Seductions – and a Critique

The End of Enlightenment: Post-Modern or Post-Secular?

John Milbank

I

Were there a post-modern, it would be the post-secular. For modernity has not been primarily, as Heidegger supposed, the 'age of the subject'. This notion alleges that what is proper to enlightenment is the capturing of divine attributes by the human: the return of substance, foundation and identity from alien, remote, transcendence to their 'real' site in the inner-wordly transcendence of the knowing subject. However, this posing of a self-sufficient, initially godless subject is merely one figure of something more crucial and decisive – namely, *the secular*. Another figure, equally 'fundamental', is the state: this also is conceived as self-sufficient and self-regulating. It possesses its law within its own given circumstances, and no longer refers itself to 'the Good', or a norm exceeding itself. Both the modern soul and the modern state are self-legible: with what they are, is given also the code to construe what they are, which is at the same time a *law*-code commanding them to perform themselves again.

But which comes first, the subject or the state? Enlightened modernity is fractured between two competing foundations. It has espoused *either* the contractual state founded on the prior free and autonomous individual, *or* the individual who is realized in his freedom only as citizen of a prior social whole. This oscillation repeats, in an immanentist guise – since soul and state are now sealed off against the transcendent – a Platonic hesitation between deciphering justice first in the soul or first in the *polis*.[1] A hesitation between the near and the far-off: *near* to me, and therefore apparently more knowable, is my self-presence and physically embodied singularity; far from me is the state, which is more plausibly total and self-sufficient, yet in its remoteness and merely functional corporeality, intrinsically 'hard to grasp'. As a starting point, the subject has an epistemological, the state an ontological advantage, and reference of one to the other is a necessary mutual supplementation which can never, of course, make up for the deficiences of both. Between the near and the far-off, how to choose?

Yet modernity early on found a way to avoid this psycho-political conspiracy. As figures of immanence, both subject and state are spatial and static: substances and essences raised above the flux of time. They have stolen from God the properties of identity, foundation, will and finality, but *not* that of infinity. The latter property can only be appropriated for the whole of *nature* in its temporal and spatial extension (if one excepts the pseudo-infinity which Hegel thought he could assign to the state, in his failed attempt to resolve the soul/city *aporia*). If nature, as infinite, is the true site for a self-regulating immanence, then one confronts a temporal and always shifting process, upon which we have no right to graft inherent purposes, essences or substances, but which apparently includes every possible variety, every possible order, disordering, and re-ordering. Although the invocation of such a temporal flux might now be characterized as 'post-modern', the epochal implication is false: already certain Renaissance philosophers, and later Baruch Spinoza, put forward such an anti-transcendent naturalism, which refuses the transcendence-within-immanence of humanist secularity.[2]

Such naturalistic immanentism is the more perfect form of modernity, atheism and the secular. For it is twice removed from metaphysical theism: once from the transcendent God, then from a semi-transcendent humanity, which tries to hold fast in the depths what was previously suspended from the heights: namely substance, identity, purpose and a hierarchy of valuation. It would seem that, for a post-secular to become possible, one must call into question the *critical* credentials of inevitable immanentism. This is what I shall presently seek to do. However, there intrudes one enormous complication, which must first be specified.

In one sense the atheism of immanentism is more marked, in another sense less so. For only the *rival* to God, the human subject, seeks to displace God and so deny him (this is why Nietzsche attributes atheism to *ressentiment* and self-delusion).[3] Immanentism, by contrast (from Spinoza to Nietzsche and Heidegger – even to Derrida and Deleuze?), effectively invokes *another* divinity which is that entire temporal-spatial process which grants us our identity from before ourselves, and thereby also undoes it. If, in fact, immanentism represents the most perfect form of 'secular closure', this closure also involves a paradoxical re-invocation of the sacred. To demonstrate this, let me return to the matter of oscillation between the near and the far-off. This not only constitutes the necessary but futile mutual supplementation of psychology and politics, but is also endemic within the entire project of metaphysics. Here the hesitation works as follows: the best candidate for 'self-present' knowledge is the knowledge I have of myself as knowing. But the best candidate for self-sufficient first 'cause-of-itself' is something remote, total, all-inclusive: 'God' or the totality of being. Where to begin, in knowledge, with myself as knowing, or God as causing? The Middle Ages took the latter option; modernity since Descartes has oscillated between the two. (Even in Descartes, an *initial* option for the priority of human knowing soon starts to come unstuck, as Jean-Luc Marion has shown.)[4] But what happens when Cartesian foundations in the knowing subject are refused? When it is realized that 'the self' is merely the trace of something which precedes it, something infinitely receding and therefore elusive? One must then abandon the modernist critical hope which refused as *transgressive* any claims to know the far-off, and sought to circumscribe a sphere of clear and certain knowledge 'close at hand'. Instead, to be critical now means (for the 'post-modern') always to re-invoke 'our' implication in the remote, and thereby to expose every claim to specifiable, close-at-hand knowledge as arbitrary suppression of this implication. In this sense the priority of the remote *returns* for immanentism: notwithstanding that it now denotes, not a distant transcendent 'object', but rather a process we did not initiate and cannot hope to command, whose total unfolding would alone decipher all our most intimate and pressing mysteries.

Bizarre as it seems, a hyper-critical thought has to make reference to and even *characterize* – however obliquely – an infinite process which is ontologically commanding and decisive. It may name this *différance*, 'deterritorialization' or 'absolute speed'. But can this hyper-critical thought really escape the aporetic hesitation between near and far that is constitutive of metaphysics as such? The answer is no: the *aporia* resurfaces in a reconfigured form. Within post-structuralism, what is ontologically primary and alone citable as 'true' is an anarchic distributive process, yet this always eludes us and can *never* be 'truly represented' – whereas 'knowledge' must confine itself to the illusory self-presence and identity of the close at hand. Knowledge *becomes* true only when it has ironically receded into an infinite distance. In this construal, the *aporia* of near/remote has only been negotiated by an ungroundable *decision* to read the ratio between the 'far-off' indeterminate and the 'present' determinate as one of aleatory in-difference. That is to say, there is no 'truth' in any fleeting presence, no 'participation' of the near in the far-off, because the remote exerts no pressure of preference – *this* way, rather than that – whether ethical or aesthetic. But the question to be posed here is: how could one *know* this? How, once one has invoked the critical priority of 'the unconscious' – of that which is always decided 'before' us, and for 'reasons' which must infinitely escape us – can one emphatically assert even the 'chaotic' character of totality, its complete indifference to discrimination? For it is simply *not* self-evident that every game of truth is but a local ritual within some more ultimate and totally random distribution. This conception can itself have only the status of one more, 'entertained' possibility. It does have a certain *epistemological* priority – for we can all at least agree that anything is possible, that the rules are infinitely variable. But this does not manifestly translate into ontological assertion: *no* actual governance is demonstrable, not even an anarchic one.

Must one therefore call into question a *merely* critical exceeding of philosophy (metaphysics)? Does this exceeding not also imply the return of the religious? In the sense that it has become *critically* manifest that to think or act at all, one must make impossible decisions concerning the relation of the absolutely distant to the temporarily present.

Spinoza tried to negotiate this *ratio* within philosophy: on the one hand he conceived of knowledge as 'near', as my increase in strength and joy in so far as I can act together *with* as many other creatures as possible. On the other hand he conceived of knowledge as 'remote', since the only completed, 'true' knowledge is the entire, infinitely realized action of the totality of being. To negotiate this gulf he spoke of 'the third kind of knowledge' as an abrupt transition from my own standpoint of acting/knowing to an intuition of the acting/knowing of *Deus/Natura*.[5] The later response of Schleiermacher (and other romantics) to this was surely correct. He followed Spinoza in dethroning the theoretical knowledge of a subject who seeks to 'encompass' objects, and the practical knowledge of a subject who seeks to legislate for himself. But beyond Spinoza he insisted that the relation of the self to totality, although critically unavoidable, admits of many possible, and transcendentally non-adjudicable determinations: therefore, he claimed, it belongs to the sphere of 'religion'.[6] Gilles Deleuze and Felix Guattari have recently claimed that what is proper to philosophy as such is the refusal of transcendence (definitory of religion) and assertion of the self-sufficiency of immanence.[7] However, if even a philosophy committed to immanence (and so most purely philosophy?) cannot critically resolve the *aporia* of the near and remote, then Schleiermacher is correct: *even* what is most proper to philosophy, the consideration of totality, is now subject to despoliation by religion – such that the philosophical elective affinity with immanence appears as just one more 'religious' preference.

The strand in modernity that *most* rebuts transcendence (within as well as beyond the world) turns out, then, not to be unequivocally 'secular'. On the contrary, by refusing the finite self-enclosure of humanism it has to trespass once again, for critical reasons, upon what should be critically out of bounds – the sacred. But can there be still, today, another rival mode of trespass which would be equally critical and yet stray as far as a genuinely transcendent 'beyond'? I want to suggest that this is possible, in the following (abbreviated) fashion.

The invocation of a creator God in Christianity and Judaism has not conformed in any straightforward way to the protocols of metaphysics or 'onto-theology' – that is to say the reference to God/Being as a *causa sui* and first cause which can be known like a kind of ultimate object by a representing subject who makes him stand at the ultimate end of an inductive/deductive chain of reasoning.[8] On the contrary, if one cites writers like Augustine, Pascal and Kierkegaard, one might say that their theological as opposed to philosophical discourse is characterized by an *intensification* of the *aporia* of near and remote, such that instead of preferring either pole it hovers (as much as post-structuralism) in a middle ground that gives rise to both 'God' and the human subject, only through a continuous dispossession of both. In this field, God can only be 'known' in so far as the subject makes a movement of love towards him, but for this love to be adequate it must be without conceivable object or finite attainment. Here, 'transcendence' certainly cannot denote the 'ideological' privileging, essentializing and absolutizing of some pre-given object, subject or order within the world; on the contrary, the world is 'flattened' in relation to something entirely beyond, categorically other and unattainable. Yet if the subject is only 'itself' in its movement towards this transcendence, in its being graciously 'claimed' by it, then this subject is never present to itself, is always determined, before itself, by the pull of love out of itself.

'Orthodox' theology, therefore, does not attempt to suppress the aporetic middle of discourse (except where contaminated by an untransposed metaphysics). It remains with the impossible necessity to determine the indeterminable ratio between the near and the remote, yet does not claim to 'know' this ratio through the power of unassisted representational understanding alone. Instead, it construes it according to its *own logos* of love as the priority of unsettling, but self-abandoning desire. Confirmation here arises not from 'looking', but from surrender and enactment.[9]

Having first argued that the 'immanentism' of post-structuralism constitutes a disguised religiosity, I have now tried to indicate a mode of affirmation of transcendence that could stake an equal claim to be 'postmodern', to arise after the death of the subject (or as a mode of this death). So we enter, beyond philosophy, beyond even 'critical theory', yet for still more hyper-critical reasons, into the supra-critical domain of theology, or rather competing theologies. Such is the post-secular, fulfilling Walter Benjamin's claim that the philosophy of the future 'would either itself be designated as theology, or would be superordinated to theology'.[10]

II

Between theologies, there are no criteria for adjudication, yet we have to judge, and to enable this, criticism is left the task of at least making more precise discriminations. I now want to venture three of my own, in the interests of decision and judgment.

First of all, immanentism is not manifestly less *dualist* than theologies of the transcendent. The 'beyond' invoked by the latter is not a beyond 'outside' this world, because 'this world' is a totalizing figure proper only to the philosophy/theology of immanence. For Christian and Jewish theology there is really no 'whole', but only the ceaseless 'arriving' of the beyond in every new temporal addition which always fulfils the self-exceeding that is love. The 'beyond' arrives again as the other before us, next to us, in front of us, like the new infant calling out from her cradle. This renders every new instance ontologically primary, not subordinate to any process which bears it – though not superior to it either. In this way a reference of each finite thing to a source 'beyond' *disallows* any dualities or hierarchical discriminations within the world.

By contrast, immanentism is fated to reascribe to duality. If 'the whole', or the entire temporal-spatial process is absolute, then even if this absolute only exists and occurs through its 'fracture' into finite instances (this being the post-Heideggerean modification of Spinozism), the whole process in its anarchy and indifference must still be 'master'. Such that *either* the particulars in their 'truth' are swallowed up as determined parts of the whole, or *else* in their self-vaunting, self-presenting 'falsity', they are at variance with the whole, refusing its point of vantage. Whereas the dualism of transcendence is, in a sense, self-cancelling, because here the finite only 'is' when it denies its finitude in its being towards the infinite source (which *as* infinite is *not* a foundational source but an always already supplemented source – only 'before' all that arrives *as* all that arrives), the dualism of immanentism *re-instates* a Platonic conflictual dualism between an eternally privileged and an inevitably self-deceiving vantage point.[11] (Here one should note that the Platonic, *metaphysical* mode of affirming transcendence, which elevates something within the world into a privileged position, itself remains, as Kierkegaard realized, locked within immanence.[12] But conversely, an immanentism claiming to be pure philosophy will always re-introduce metaphysical transcendence.)

Secondly, immanentism does *not* more manifestly delete the subject than theologies of the transcendent. To grasp this point, one must first recognize that post-structuralism deconstructs not just the subject, but rather the subject/object duality in its mutual complicity and confirmation. Instead of this duality it posits every *ens* as a kind of subject/body – so, for example, insisting in the wake of Bergson that every physical movement involves also an 'image' or signifying representation of the earlier by the later instance.[13] To abolish the subject is to disallow the primacy of mirroring representation (theory) and of the domination of the inert by the free (practice); yet what replaces this is a highly 'subjectivized' universe, or one in which every *ens* is defined by its unique configuration in relation to other *ens* and its capacity for spontaneous and creative reconfiguration (a capacity which allows and requires 'representation', but ensures that it can never represent *except* as 'otherwise'). There is an infinite chain of acting/acted-upon subject-bodies, whose most complex entanglement we name 'humanity'.

The 'subjectivization' of reality genuinely comes 'after' the demise of the human subject. However, at the level of totality, of the invocation of an aleatory absolute, post-structuralism has to *deny* the primacy of the relation of subject/body to subject/body. For we do not, according to Deleuze and Guattari, relate to 'the absolute' (Deterritorialization)[14] as another subject-body, or the infinite 'arrival' of subject/bodies, but instead through our underlying identity as *thinking* being (*res cogitans*!) with this 'infinite speed'.[15] The latter is both *physis* and *logos*, and lies beyond relation, since the infinite speed of actuality is defined by the immediate and complete 'return' of this movement which is *logos* – imperfectly 'delayed' in *our* understanding. Therefore at the level of absolute 'chaos', truth as perfect self-presence and representation is restored to its primacy, and the primacy of the love-relation – where the otherness of the other who is desired must exceed the reach of knowledge – is refused. But what is more, the *philosopher* is one who gives priority to his identity with this absolute. It is he who claims (by adversion to the 'pre-philosophical' assumption of a 'plane of immanence') that the inter-relations of subject/bodies (or singularities/events in Deleuze's terminology) are only possible as confinements of infinite speed. But is not the latter an *object*? Albeit one merely traceable, and scarcely representable. And is not the philosopher self-defined by ironic withdrawal from the flux, and so by his self-assertion as *knowing* subject? Aspiring to represent, and *not* primarily to act and love. Within philosophy, the remote has always been characterized as an object, and as something attainable through reflective knowledge, precisely because it is conceived as the far boundary of an immanent totality. Therefore for Deleuze to make the gesture of commitment to philosophy and immanence is inevitably to decide to remain *with* the subject (if only *as* philosopher) in precisely the sense that post-structuralism purportedly seeks to overcome.

On the other hand, theologies of the transcendent can logically *remain with* the ultimacy of the interrelations of subject/bodies. (Though they need to rid themselves – following the early lead of Tertullian – of the metaphysical residue of characterizing God as '*spirit*' rather than matter.) They can do so, since they construe the relation of the individual to the absolute, not as the problematical coincidence of nature with identity, but rather as 'somewhat like' the love relation of subject/body to subject/body. If, in such a relation, it is always the case that the subject is partially given to herself by the other, then in the case of a creator God this is maximized – even my most active and free being is none other than the love of God for me.

In the third place, immanentism is *not* manifestly more peaceful in its implications. On the face of it the case against appeals to transcendence is severe: does this not always absolutize the violence of the *victor*, concealing it with a sacred gloss? But this could only be true of false, 'metaphysical' transcendence. Whereas the case against immanence is irremediable. Its own advocates do not seek to disguise their vision of an ontological agonism. For where every assertion is arbitrary, where every insinuation of stable presence can only succeed by suppressing the flux which subtends it, then violence can never be overcome, and the best possible mode of political resistance is an asymptotic but realizable approximation to 'infinite speed' (and the dire peace of anarchic self-identity). Again, the site of post-structuralism turns out to be merely philosophical and Platonic after all: the philosopher-king can only instantiate 'truth' (deterritorialization) in the state at the cost of betraying it. And peace may be contemplated, yet never performed.

Where, as for post-structuralism, the ontological difference between Being and beings is characterized by violent rupture and subterfuge, then this must also categorize every ordinary transition between being and being, for the ontological difference only arises (for immanentism) in and through these transitions. And yet it seems that this discourse is in rapid retreat from such a politically unacceptable conclusion. Derrida himself now talks of the irretrievable trace, not in terms of rupture, but rather (echoing Levinas) of our pre-ordination to responsibility for an anonymous 'other' who ineluctably instigates 'me' before 'I' have fully arrived.[16] However, this new turn may be more hopeful than coherent. A determintion of the trace as love rather than rupture cannot be *critically* accomplished. Objectively 'the call' is indeed anonymous, and betokens anything we like. Identifying the caller (and how could one not always have already done this?) as immanent Being, or alternatively as the other in the trace of the transcendent God, is rather a matter of 'religious' decision.

Even the Levinasian attempt first of all to understand the ethical pre-religiously as our 'sacrificial' and unlimited 'responsibility' for an uncharacterizable other, whose personhood always recedes behind her phenomenal appearance, proves incoherent and inadequate. For this approach confines itself within an unjustifiable transcendental assertion of a noumenal sphere which permits the ethical relation to determine *a priori* all theoretical knowledge. This claim to 'demonstrate' the priority of the ethical simultaneously confines the ethical to an empty 'pre-ontological' formalism. This is a formalism which occludes the *political* truth that, prior to the question of admitting the demands of the other, or nurturing her if she has been injured, arises the question of distributive justice, of how, concretely, we can shape our collective lives as a kind of musical harmony in which – despite and through movement – everything finds a 'proper' place, even though there is no law or rule for arbitrating 'placement'. In semi-recognition of this, Levinas, like Kant before him, has now moved away from the question of 'dyadic' mutual recognition to that of 'triadic' judgment (once there are *two* others, one must discriminate and divide). Also to the question of the embodiment of 'the ought' in Being.[17] But this is precisely the point at which, for Levinas as already for Kant, ethics must self-exceed itself towards religion.[18] Purportedly to discover an immanent 'subjective' realm, apart from being, governed before our decision by ethical laws (Levinas's first move) proves vapid. This for the simple reason that to will the good, to will responsibility for the neighbour, is empty, unless it be possible that there can *be* the good, that it can be incarnate (thereby *alone* real) in bodily life. Therefore to will that there should be the good is also to have faith that reality is infinitely receptive to the good, or that being can entertain (exhaustively) peaceful co-existence and mutual consumptions that are gift and reception, not spoliation and submission.

We can never *know* this, but only believe it. Hence for both Kant and Levinas there is a point at which ethical willing demands that one construe reality as 'finally' the embodiment of a peacefully granted gift, in order for us to be able to assume that it may become the site of *our* peaceful giving. Where this construal is made, then every instance of violent rupture is reduced to non-essential contingency and inhibition of existence.

Thus I want to claim, even a purely critical discrimination exposes the agonism of the immanentist vision, and by contrast discloses the Jewish/Christian invocation of transcendence as the only possible vehicle for the sustaining of political hope. But of course it canot force faith, nor constrain our choice.

Notes

1. See Plato, *Republic*, Books II to IV, esp. II, 368d. In the latter place, near and remote are inverted – the city is nearer and more 'legible', and the soul further off and more obscure.
2. See Yirmiyahu Yovel, *Spinoza and Other Heretics*, Princeton, NJ 1989; Hans Blumenberg, *The Legitimacy of the Modern Age*, Cambridge, Mass. 1985, 457–597.
3. Friedrich Nietzsche, *Thus Spake Zarathustra*, Harmondsworth 1969, 275–9.
4. Jean-Luc Marion, *Sur le Prisme Métaphysique de Descartes*, Paris 1986, 97–137, 371–8.
5. Baruch Spinoza, *Ethics*, Part V; Gilles Deleuze, *Spinoza: Practical Philosophy*, San Francisco 1988, 79–83.
6. Friedrich Schleiermacher, *On Religion*, Cambridge 1988, 'Second Speech', 96–140.
7. Gilles Deleuze and Felix Guattari, *Qu'est ce que La Philosophie?*, Paris 1991, 38–50.
8. See Jean-Luc Marion, *God Without Being*, Chicago 1991.
9. Critique of a dominant visual metaphor for self-understanding and relationship to God is already implicit in Augustine's *Confessions*, Books I–VI. See also Marion, *Sur le Prisme* (n.4), 293–371 (on Pascal).
10. Walter Benjamin, 'On the Programme of the Coming Philosophy', in Gary Smith (ed.), *Benjamin*, Chicago 1990.
11. See my 'Problematizing the Secular: the Post-Postmodern Agenda', in Philippa Berry and Andrew Wernick (ed.), *The Shadow of Spirit* (London, forthcoming).
12. Søren Kierkegaard, *The Concept of Anxiety*, Princeton, NJ 1980, 80–110.
13. Henri Bergson, *Matter and Memory*, New York 1991; Gilles Deleuze, *Cinema I. The Movement-Image*, London 1986.
14. Gilles Deleuze and Felix Guattari, *A Thousand Plateaus*, London 1988, 109–10.
15. Deleuze and Guattari, *Qu'est ce que La Philosophie?* (n.7), 41.
16. Jacques Derrida, '"Eating Well", or the calculation of the subject', in *Who comes after the Subject?*, ed. Eduardo Cadava et al., London 1991, 96–120.
17. Emmanuel Levinas, *Otherwise than Being or Beyond Essence*, The Hague 1981, esp. 153–65. And see Marion, *God without Being* (n.8). Marion's version of the 'pre-ontological' is more convincing than Levinas', because it is characterized not as responsibility, but as love or 'free gift', which is always the gift *of* being. Yet one might want to ask Marion, is love as gift really 'before' love as relation (and therefore ontological)? Or is each somehow before the other, and does the doctrine of the Trinity convey precisely this? The Son is only generated through the Spirit's procession; the Spirit is gift of the love of Father and Son.
18. Immanuel Kant, *Critique of Judgment*, 'Appendix' id., *Religion Within the Bounds of Reason Alone*, New York 1960, preface, p.5.

Between Praxis and Theory: Theology in a Crisis over Orientation

Werner G. Jeanrond

Theology today is criticized from many sides, no longer just from 'outside', i.e. by representatives of disciplines and attitudes which are opposed to it, but also from 'within', from the ranks of theologians themselves. Among those who are against theology there are sometimes very opposed types of criticism. This group first, of course, includes traditional atheists, although in decreasing numbers, but it also increasingly includes Christians who have had a theological training but have lost confidence that present-day theological thought has any constructive contribution to make. However, even among theologians who still think that theology is intrinsically meaningful and full of promise, there is strong criticism both of the organization of theology as it is carried on at present in the universities of Europe and North America, and also of the method of theological thought in modernity and post-modernity.

In this article I shall limit myself to discussing the arguments of those groups which affirm the Christian religion but indicate that they have considerable doubts about present-day Christian theology. I shall be concerned with the question what basis there still is for critical and self-critical theology in the face of such criticism.

I. Religion, yes – theology, no?

The decline of religion long prophesied by Marxists has not come about. On the contrary, the collapse of Marxist-atheist systems in Europe has been followed by a growing interest in religious practice. However, this more marked interest in religion in the Christian West has yet to lead to any detectably greater move towards theological reflection. Rather, the recent absence of any possibility of discussions between theologians and

Marxist-atheist thinkers has furthered the isolation of theological thinking even more. Theological faculties, institutes, professorial chairs and academies largely continue to exist under the protection of decrees from state and church, but any impulses which emanate from them are seldom perceptible among the wider public. Granted, liberation theology, feminist theology and ecological theology still meet with widespread public interest, but interestingly, at the same time such theologies are deepening the suspicion that there is something wrong with the traditional so-called 'critical' university theology of the twentieth century. Moreover, the concerns of all the three theological trends that I have mentioned have not arisen from theological thought itself, but have been picked up relatively late by individual theologians from a wider public discussion.

It seems that theology is lagging behind cultural developments generally, is simply reacting, and is no longer able to communicate traditional material on which it has reflected in the cultural pluralism of our time. Especially now that the old world order of the Cold War has collapsed and there are no plans for the future anywhere, we hear hardly anything that is really new from theologians either.[1] Theological contributions to a future world order can only rarely be detected in current discussion.[2] Has theology been shunted into an intellectual siding? Is it significant that nowadays leading theologians are concerned more with hermeneutical and methodological questions than with concrete plans from a Christian perspective for a universal world order? So is theology more than ever concerned with itself, rather than with the tasks for a global future?

Thus while a re-religionizing of people is taking place world wide, Roman Catholic theology is not alone in presenting a confused picture: and what it lacks is not intellectual equipment, but a theological strategy as to how its specific thought material can be communicated afresh to our world. This is partly connected with the fact that the traditional channels by which theological influence is exerted, namely the link between theology and the world through the church, have now been blocked, at least for critical theologians within the Roman Catholic church. How did this situation come about?

II. Church, yes – theology, with reservations?

Granted, in the history of the church the relationship between theologians and the authorities has never been free from tensions. Nevertheless, today it has to be said that there is a remarkably deep gulf in the Catholic church between critical theology and the leadership of the church.[3] Unfortunately the greater trust which had developed between bishops and theologians during the Second Vatican Council has long since been undermined again.

Critical theology, critical challenges to the church's teaching authority and the discussion of criteria for true authority in the church are not what many bishops want today. Indeed one can even see how it is that those Catholics whose doubts about the need for critical theology are all too clearly known are being nominated bishops.

The collapse of concerted action between critical theology and the church leaders has deprived of a church public all those theologians who ever want to express any constructive criticism. Either they have already been affected by the ban of church censorship or the general climate of censorship has already weakened their will to speak out. The theologians still courted by the magisterium are almost without exception those who no longer want to engage in critical activity or have already taken an oath not to do so. Given this situation, it might be more appropriate to distinguish between court theologians, critical theologians and anxious theologians. The first are concerned with the training of priests and the justification and continuation of the church's power structures; the last have been forced to the periphery of the church or beyond by either having been refused the church's permission to teach or having had this withdrawn, without any public reason; and the silent middle no longer plays any public role.

This situation means that critical theologians who do not have the fortune to teach in institutions which have no ties with the church can still get a hearing for their theology only through the mass media, and this in turn is held against them by the magisterium as being *hybris* or capriciousness. But the mass media and many other critics of the day are in turn more interested in the scandal of the treatment and marginalization of some critical theologians than in the responsible communication of theological insights and ideas. So what kind of a public is still left for critical theology?

This question is all the more important, since many Catholic theologians still cherish the illusion that outside the academic world there is still a large public seriously interested in theological questions and sufficiently educated to cope with them. However, the sales figures for theological literature hardly support that. At any rate in the industrial nations, there has not yet been any breakthrough of theological education on a wide scale, either in the church or outside it. Yet one cannot claim that there is in principle no interest in theological thought; rather, it is the channels of theological communication which need to be renewed or recreated.

The three publics for theology which have been termed by David Tracy the academy, society and the church[4] may exist for many Protestant theologians, but for Catholic theologians they are there only to a very limited degree: court theologians may still be listened to by the government of the church, but often they can no longer find a serious hearing in the academy and in society. Critical theologians are deprived of room in the church, at any rate of that room in the church which is still effectively controlled by the *magisterium*, though they may perhaps be able to find some hearing in the academy and in society. And those theologians who keep silent deprive themselves of any room.

But what about those theological developments which today have a high profile for the wider public?

III. Praxis, yes – theory, no?

The development of Latin American liberation theology and its forerunner, European political theology, has again reminded theological discussion of the difficult relationship between theory and praxis. There was probably never any serious doubt that theology must essentially be concerned with problems of human praxis, but there is at present considerable disagreement about the nature of the relationship between the two theological factors. That theology, in the words of Karl Rahner, always moves at a particular level of reflection, which is distinct from religious experiences, though it is motivated by them and directed towards them, is important for its understanding of itself as a discipline.[5] Otherwise theology could not be of any service in clarifying, comparing and generally criticizing these experiences for an interested public. So political theology and liberation theology do not primarily put in doubt the purpose of theology to be reflection; what they put in doubt is, first, the traditional framework of reflection and, secondly, the methods of theological reflection in the modern world.

Some years ago, Johann Baptist Metz commented in connection with the situation of theology and the methods of doing theology in the modern world, first, that both a world-less theology and also an uncritical theology of the world conflicted with the Christian message and, secondly, that theological thought cannot be simply identical with Enlightenment thought.[6] As an alternative, Metz outlines a 'practical fundamental theology' which seeks to overcome the aporias of the Enlightenment by attacking 'an undialectical subordination of praxis to theory and idea'. 'It insists on the intelligible power of praxis itself, in the sense of a dialectic between theory and praxis. To this degree it does theology under the "primacy of praxis".'[7] These clarifications must still be taken into consideration today, because they contradict all those who would like to rob such praxis of the possibility of and the need for reflection. Metz indefatigably insists on the dialectical character of his political theology, for which the conditions for liberating and responsible action lie specifically in the relationship between praxis and reflection. So Metz is not concerned to liberate theology from critical thought but to direct theological thought towards a discussion of the possibilities of and needs for action which arise out of the Christian call to discipleship communicated by means of a narrative.[8]

In principle the Latin American liberation theologians follow a similar line. While Gustavo Gutiérrez criticizes Metz for not making any analyses of more concrete situations, he praises his fertile attempt 'to think the faith through. It takes into consideration the political dimension of the faith and is indeed aware of the most pervasive and acute problems which persons encounter today.'[9] Thus neither Metz nor liberation theology as such criticize the possibility of theology, but merely call for theological thought to pay attention to the concerns of politics or liberation.

But at this point some doubts arise. First there is the question how we are to understand the 'intelligible power of praxis itself'. Is this a possibility of reflection which outdoes the freedom of critical thought achieved with so much toil by modernity and the Enlightenment, or does the intelligible power of praxis itself need an institutionalized criticism which traces in a scientific way the many interpretations of Christian religion in history and the present? Secondly, there is need for a discussion as to how Christian action can be preserved from lapsing into a more or less blind activism, however well meant, which occasionally seems to be heralded by the second generation of liberation theologians. And thirdly, it must be asked whether Christian theology is really only legitimate when it prescribes directly and completely the various concerns of political and social emancipation.[10]

The last question also relates to the discussion of the horizon of feminist and ecological thought in theology. Of course the unmasking and overcoming of patriarchal domination in religion and society is an urgent concern. And new reflection on the organic interaction of human life with all the other dimensions of our universe is equally urgent.[11] However, a critical understanding of theology does not take it for granted that theological thought should be identified with attention to one or more of these really important concerns.[12]

Such one-sided attachments of theological thought to particular needs for action have contributed to theology having lost its reputation as a critical discipline in some quarters. So such doubt in the breadth of interest of theological thought is nourished not only by clerical fixations but also by a narrowing of interest in theological argument itself.

Now we must not accuse such representatives of political theology and liberation theology as Metz and Gutiérrez of having encouraged such narrowings of theological thought. But we have to recognize that they have not put up sufficient resistance to such narrowings, particularly by having failed to emphasize the critical heritage of Enlightenment thought clearly enough in their methodology. To hold fast to this heritage does not, of course, involve taking on all the aporias of the Enlightenment. On the contrary, the valid repudiation by Metz of a bourgeois theology purely related to the subject is indebted to this critical tradition. Moreover on the side of post-modern philosophy the discussion of the concept of the subject in modernity has meanwhile gone further. Theology cannot evade a critical discussion with the post-subjective tradents of human thought and action. The dialectic between praxis and theory must continually be clarified afresh in this process of critical discussion with post-modern patterns of thought and action.

IV. Ways out of the crisis?

Theology will preserve its theo-logical identity and meet with the public interest it deserves if it does not allow itself to be absorbed by any activity, however important, and instead once again puts the question of God under the conditions of its particular present. Granted, the question of God may not be divorced from considerations of appropriate action, but it may not be identified with such considerations either (cf. Matt. 22.37–40). Otherwise critical detachment and a recognition of the limits of human thought, love and action will be blurred.[13] In this way, for Christian theology which asserts this distance, a room for critical and self-critical thought will be opened up in which, first, all hermeneutical theories of the interpretation of reality can be discussed and applied and, secondly, the discussion of the most appropriate interpretation of the Christian tradition and of present possibilities for thought and action can be encouraged.

Of course, such an appropriate interpretation of past and present reality must stand in an authentic dialectical relationship with the manifold praxis of human experience. But this dialectic calls for honest mutual criticism, and that presupposes that Christian ideas for action must lay claim to the distance between reflection and immediate action which is necessary for this dialectic. That is true not only for dialogue at the different levels of church commitment, but also for dialogue at every level of society generally and of academic discussion in particular.[14] Critical theology cannot withdraw or easily allow itself to be displaced from any of these spheres of thought and action.

Probably no single theologian will be in a position to operate with the same power at all these public levels. So it is nonsensical to condemn some theologians for concentrating on critical discussions in particular public spheres. Any theological creed framed too narrowly, no matter what its provenance, which seeks to bind the individual theologian to a particular view of faith or the world or to oblige the theologian to adopt one particular option for action, must be rejected as an ideology. Instead of such hasty condemnation of colleagues, it would seem much more promising to get honest dialogue among theologians going again and thus encourage critical discussion with our Christian tradition and with all the dimensions of our world. Only this critical discussion can create a basis on which theologians can hopefully pursue the question of God and the principles and strategies for appropriate action with one another and with any other interested parties.

Translated by John Bowden

Notes

1. Marion Gräfin Dönhoff's complaint in 'Wenn der Wille zum Handeln fehlt: Der ratlose Westen vergibt eine grosse Chance', *Die Zeit* 17 (17 April 1991), 1, on the present vacuum in the Western world, can also be applied to theology.
2. Hans Küng's *Global Responsibility*, London and New York 1991, is an honourable exception.
3. There is an extended discussion of this development in Gabriel Daly, 'Catholicism and Modernity', *Journal of the American Academy of Religion* 53, 1985, 773–96.
4. Cf. David Tracy, *The Analogical Imagination: Christian Theology and the Culture of Pluralism*, New York and London 1981, 3–31.
5. Karl Rahner, *Foundations of Christian Faith. Introduction to the Idea of Christianity*, New York and London 1978, 20–2.
6. Johann Baptist Metz, *Glaube in Geschichte und Gesellschaft: Studien zu einer praktischen Fundamentaltheologie*, Mainz 1977.
7. Ibid., 47.
8. See also Matthew Lamb, 'The Dialectics of Theory and Praxis within Paradigm Analysis', in Hans Küng and David Tracy (eds.), *Paradigm Change in Theology*, Edinburgh 1989, 63–109.
9. Gustavo Gutiérrez, *Theology of Liberation*, Maryknoll and London ²1988, 129f.
10. Cf. Werner G. Jeanrond, 'Towards a Critical Theology of Christian Praxis', *The Irish Theological Quarterly* 51, 1985, 16–45.
11. The connection between feminist and ecological concerns is stressed particularly by Anne Primavesi, *From Apocalypse to Genesis: Ecology, Feminism and Christianity*, Tunbridge Wells, Kent 1991; and by Katherine Zappone, *The Hope for Wholeness: A Spirituality for Feminists*, Dublin and Mystic, CT 1991.
12. There are clear hints of an identification of feminist criticism with a universal project e.g. in Zappone, *Hope for Wholeness* (n.11), 10: 'Although feminism originates in *women's* awareness and critical rejection of their oppressive experience in patriarchal society, its parameters expand to include concern for all of humanity and life in the natural world. At the heart of the feminist project, then, lies the collective imagination of a new world and a new way of being-in-the-world.'
13. David Tracy stresses this distinction in *Plurality and Ambiguity: Hermeneutics, Religion, Hope*, San Francisco and London 1987, as follows: 'Christian salvation is not exhausted by any program of political liberation, to be sure, but Christian salvation,

rightly understood, cannot be divorced from the struggle for total human liberation – individual, social, political and religious.'

14. Tracy has presented a theory of conversation which takes account of the postmodern situation of thought in his work *Plurality and Ambiguity* (n.13).

The Reciprocal Exclusiveness of Modernity and Religion among Contemporary Thinkers: Jürgen Habermas and Marcel Gauchet

Anne Fortin-Melkevik

Introduction

The thinkers of modernity, from Kant to Max Weber, radicalize the fundamental problem of the reciprocal exclusion of faith and reason and restrict the practice of theology to the sphere of that which is not knowledge and has no rationality. Modernity envisages this relationship in terms of the progressive extinction of religion itself and of religious experience. We shall be studying the problem of the reciprocal exclusiveness of modernity and religion through two post-Weberian authors, Jürgen Habermas and Marcel Gauchet, who offer diametrically opposed solutions to the problem of the survival of religious experience in modernity. However, I shall be questioning the reading of religious experience by these authors, asking what (pre)hermeneutical definition of experience they use.

I. The irresistible movement of secularization according to Habermas

According to Habermas, the movement of secularization is based on a triple process of the transformation of society.

First of all, the rationalization of images from the mystical world from which Christian religion procedes provokes the epistemological erosion of the very foundation of every religious and metaphysical conception of the world. From myth to religious and metaphysical thought and down to secularized modernity, the process of differentiation of thought and the spheres of knowledge which organize it has broken up the unity of mediaeval knowledge. Science, morality and art will no longer be founded on the metaphysical and religious conception of the world; they will become spheres of autonomous knowledge and develop their own epistemological foundations without making any recourse to a religious legitimacy. Since in modernity the religious conception of the world can no longer offer the possibility of recourse to the divine or to the cosmos to legitimate itself as the foundation of other knowledge, it will no longer be the foundation of all the modes of knowing. Rather, it will be relegated to the rank of that which is not knowledge, and put in the individual sphere of experience and subjective opinion.

This loss of epistemological legitimacy by the religious and by theological discourse over against the positive sciences has discredited any claim to truth which the religious order could make: by what right could theology sustain a truth about the world which would contradict scientific discoveries? From now on its sole areas of legitimacy will be in the sphere of subjectivity, and it will increasingly find a place alongside the dimension of aesthetic experience, to which it will be assimilated. Rather than being discourse with scientific pretensions, with modernity theology finds itself imprisoned within epistemological limits defined from the point of view of the natural sciences.

The second logical stage of the movement of secularization consists in the loss of the social function of integration which religion once had. With the dissolution of religious knowledge so that it ceases to be knowledge, this social function loses its theoretical foundation. However, the function remains, and from now on will be assumed by secular ethics (Weber) and by language which becomes the cornerstone of social consensus – replacing the rites of pre-modern societies (Durkheim).

The third logical stage of secularization will produce the utter disappearance of religious experience and all its content. By making the *social function* of religion disappear, secularization will also make the *content* of religion disappear: its outdated content, of the order of myth, cannot resist the progressive rationalization of the world's images. However, some positive aspects of religion could be recovered by the rationalization of the world's images. The process of rationalization would in fact progressively absorb the contents of myth and religion, bringing them together under a 'demythologized' aspect. Thus communicational reality would incorporate the positive content of religion in a non-dogmatic and non-ideological way.

This content, which Habermas does not expand on further – at most he mentions the idea of brotherhood – is 'transcended' above all by the ethics of communication. Ethics is in fact the sole authority which can regain for religion some of its content without, however, sharing in its supposedly dogmatic character. The traditional views of the world 'are transformed into ethics and subjective beliefs which assure the private obligatory character of modern orientations in respect of values (the "Protestant ethic")'.[1]

Habermas explains this triple process of secularization within a resume of Durkheimian theory in the light of the 'linguistic shift' of the social sciences. Thus new light is shed on the progressive rationalization of the world's images of the kind outlined by Weber by its insertion into a logic of 'communicational liquidation of a basic religious consensus'. In fact, for Habermas in his *Theory of Communicative Action*, the 'functions of social integration and expression, first fulfilled by ritual practice, pass over into communicative action: from there the authority of the sacred is progressively replaced by the authority of a (linguistic) consensus'.[2] That is why, following Durkheim, Habermas conceives that 'a social integration by faith is replaced by an *integration brought about by a mutual accord and a co-operation due to communication*' (317).

The idea of *putting the sacred into language* serves as a tool for Habermas to 'decode the *logic* of the change of form of social integration' (103, author's italics) brought out by Durkheim. In moving from the sphere of the sacred to the sphere of communicative practice, the 'functions of cultural reproduction, social integration and socialization' (103) profoundly modify the structure of the interaction: there is a move from a community of religious faith 'which simply *makes possible* social co-operation' to a *communicative community* primarily '*subject* to constraints on co-operation' (103). Here the emphasis is on the conditions underlying the co-operation: the community of religious faith makes co-operation possible in an incidental way and as though by accident. This is an unforeseen secondary effect. For the communicative community, by contrast, co-operation represents the very condition of its possibility. As an obligatory vector ordering the action, co-operation so to speak plays the role of an *idea of reason*. Primarily structured by ritual practice, this co-operation thus proves progressively to be ruled by language. Then only,

> the potential of rationality present in the action orientated on intercomprehension could be detached and converted into a rationalization of the worlds experienced by social groups to the degree that the *language* fulfils the functions of intercomprehension, co-ordination of action and socialization of individuals, thus becoming a medium through which cultural reproduction, social integration and socialization are achieved (98, my italics).

Thus the language which structures communicative interaction will become the authority where the 'energies of social solidarity' are connected (67), making useless and out of date the authority of the ritual practice which formerly guaranteed this role.

However, there is an ambiguity in Habermas's theory. This relates to the theoretical status to be accorded to the disappearance of religion:

> (Religion in Habermas) suffers the fate that the Enlightenment reserved for it: that of a vision from the outmoded world, the moral idea of which (the idea of brotherhood) it is hardly possible still to take over. But if Habermas himself sees the roots of an undistorted world of experience in the religious traditions of the world, it is hard to see how these traditions, particularly that of brotherhood, can be evacuated at this point: is it *de facto* (secularization leaves religion behind it) or *de jure* (the inconsistency of the religious image of the world)?[3]

Habermas does not respond to this objection directly, but in my view he would opt for the second response. In fact for Habermas, as Marcel Gauchet puts it, 'the religious cannot survive the secularization of its contents' in the modern age. From now on religion proves powerless to explain the world, and at most it can survive in the private sphere, where the status of the explanations of the world that it is capable of providing will be of a 'fantastic' or 'imaginary' order.

That, then, is the irreversible and even necessary way in which, for Habermas, the loss of the social function of religion as providing integration will lead to the end of the religious. He has no regrets about this, since the 'tendency to the rational' which is implied in this secularization will at all events have opened up a way of recovering and integrating the positive dimensions of religion. Language will assume in a *more rational* way the social function which religion fulfilled.

So Habermas envisages religion only from the perspective of its social function, and only gives a *structural* definition: religion allows cultural reproduction, integration and socialization. Consequently the social function of integration will persist, but religion as an agent will disappear. Without really dwelling on the *content* of religion, Habermas deduced from the loss of the social *function* of religion the supplanting, pure and simple, of its contents, thus making the end of religion inevitable.

II. From the social function of the religious to the subjective function of religious experience: Marcel Gauchet

It is not my intention here to give a detailed summary of the thesis which Marcel Gauchet puts forward in his book *The Disenchantment of the World*,[4] but simply to discuss the function of religion. Contrary to

Habermas, who sees in the disappearance of the social function of religion the suppression of all religion under every aspect, Marcel suggests that the social function of religion will be replaced by the subjective function of religious experience. Theologians cannot ignore this new approach.

A definition of religion

The first level of definition of religion that one would expect from the sociologist Marcel Gauchet is of course the political level. This is the option that he chooses in conceiving of religion as that which 'organizes the human social field' as 'structure' and as 'culture' (11). In an almost obligatory way, we might say, religion is defined as a *'historical* phenomenon' (10, author's italics), i.e. is defined 'by a beginning and an end . . . corresponding to a precise age of humanity which is succeeded by another' (ibid).

However, these definitions are not the only ones that Gauchet favours. His book derives its logic from an ontological definition of religion. At least, that is what is suggested by the use which Gauchet does not hesitate to make of the concept of the essence of the religious:

> The essence of the religious is everything in this operation: the establishment of a relationship of dispossession between the universe of visible human beings and its foundation (11).

More precisely, the essence of the religious consists in alienation, in 'the institutionalization of *man against himself*', in a 'relationship of negativity of social man to himself' (10, author's italics). 'The radical dispossession, the integral otherness of the foundation is original' (12). The archaic societies are those in which one finds this essence of religion in its pure state; they have been the most structured by the religious, looking to a mythical origin set outside human reach.

For Gauchet, the relationship to the time of the origin which fixes the present in a repetition of 'what has been founded once for all' (15), this block on social innovation, justified by commands received from the gods, ancestors or heroes (13), is in fact 'the key to the relationship between religion and society and the secret of the nature of the religious' (15).

So Gauchet postulates an ideal, 'pure', plenary state of religion. He puts it 'at the beginning, in this world before the state. I have allowed myself to form a concrete picture of it from some special areas where it has survived, in America and in New Guinea' (x). It is on this precise point that the whole originality of his thesis turns: it reverses the evolutionist trajectory of religion that some historicism had suggested was necessary. Whereas this history of religions had constructed a scheme within which the universal religions represented the full development of the idea of religion (an idea which would only have been contained in embryo in the primitive religions), Gauchet asserts the contrary: 'where religion is concerned, what looks like progress is a decline', since the perfection of religion comes at the beginning and not in the 'universal religions', which are 'no more than stages in its slackening' (xi).

For Marcel Gauchet, the end of religion relates to the social function of religion and its structuring of 'material, social and mental life' (133). This function declines progressively under the effect of the emancipation of society from religious authority, when the society and the individual disengage themselves from religious subjection to achieve autonomy.

Christianity as a 'departure from religion'

While postulating that the nature of the religious bond is in essence incompatible with the autonomy of the individual, Gauchet sees in Christianity the religion which allows 'the departure from religion' (11). The achievement of political autonomy is primarily indicated in the very principles of this religion. Departing from the essence of religion, Christianity contains within itself principles which make it possible to conquer religious alienation. These principles are those of the transcendence of God and the separation of this world and its foundation. The liberation of this space of transcendence allows the creation of the sphere of legality over against the sphere of sociality: the *de jure* is no longer mixed in with the *de facto*.

The subjective function of religious experience

This departure from religion explains the reason for the end of religion: the fact that society takes its destiny into its hands frees it from alienation and the dispossession of its religious foundation. The social function of religion, which was to maintain society in total dependence on the order established by the gods, now becomes outmoded. Contrary to Habermas, who had banished to oblivion a religion stripped of any social function, Gauchet has religion disappearing in order to be recovered in a better way at the level of individual experience.

> Must not the disappearance of the basic *social function* of the religious normally end up by leading to a loss or an erosion of the very possibility of a belief – perhaps very slow, but inexorable? One might be tempted to think so. Except that here one is faced with another problem which significantly complicates things: that of the *subjective function* which religious experience keeps – or acquires – when its social function is obliterated (236, my italics).

Today there is nothing left of the role of religion in structuring material, social and mental life 'except individual experiences and systems of convictions' (133). Habermas saw in the systems of convictions which survived religion the basis for an entirely secularized ethics, a communicative ethics. For Gauchet, things are different: rather than a passage from one function to another, here we have an illustration of the 'faculty of a religious type of experience for individuals' (134) with anthropological roots, like an 'original nucleus of potential religiousness, both logical and psychological' (ibid). Gauchet does not see this faculty as the heart of religion, or as a permanent feeling which would allow the relativizing of religious history, but as a kind of irreducible anthropological remnant.

The dimension of subjective experience of a religious kind which subsists as a 'subjective anchorage for the spirit of religion' (111) is detached from all content. In fact this content, which was bound up with the social function of religion, will be dissolved at the same time as religion. The 'ineradicable subjective stratum of the religious phenomenon' which is the foundation of the religious experience would be beyond all content, anterior to any explicit formulation in a religion. Hence, for Gauchet, the mistake of those who want to justify the existence of religion as a manifestation of this subjective experience: no 'unavoidable need of religion' on the basis of a recognition of the impossibility of eliminating religious experience (292). Gauchet dissociates the experience which he himself describes as 'religious' from the sphere of religion, thus making it available for a new framework, that of the aesthetic dimension:

> The subjective experience from which in fact the religious systems derive can in some ways function perfectly by itself, in a void. It has no need to project itself in fixed representations, articulated in a body of doctrine and shared socially, in order to have an effect ... It can very well invest itself elsewhere than in the type of practice and discourse which so far have been its chosen terrain (292, my italics).

However, rather than follow the manifestations of religious experience in the many 'elsewheres' in which it invests itself today,[5] Gauchet takes a course which consists in disengaging the theoretical structure of this 'anthropological substrate' through three 'levels' at which this substrate plays the role of a 'structuring scheme for experience' (293), three levels which structure all human experience, 'three relics of religion' which were the characteristics of what was once called religious experience.

The 'relics of religion'

The first and last relics of religion relate to 'the demand of human thought itself which feels all reality from two aspects, that of this world and that of indifferentiation, and the experience of the problem that we are for ourselves' (ibid.). I shall consider only the second structure through which religious experience survives, namely aesthetic experience.

Aesthetic experience is subjected to an 'analysis of the same order' as the two other structures through which religious experience survives. Thus whereas the experience of indifferentiation relates to 'the way of thinking about the profound nature of things', aesthetic experience relates to 'the way of receiving their appearance, the imaginary organization of our grasp of the world'; it is the 'faculty for imagining reality, and no longer our faculty of intellection' (296). Aesthetic experience is said to be the experience of the sacred, 'of the presence of the divine in the world', the 'irruption of the wholly other in the familiarity of things' (297).[6] An experience of difference, the ordeal of a break, aesthetic experience, presents the world to us as 'open to a mystery that we do not know' (297) and opens itself up as a mediation of the sacred.

> The sacred is specifically the presence of absence ... a tangible manifestation of what is normally hidden from the senses and removed from human grasp. And art, in the specific sense in which we other moderns understand it, *is the continuation of the sacred by other means* (ibid., my italics).

The difference, otherness, depth, can now only be sought within the limits of this world, which since the end of religion relates only to itself. From now on art will assume the role of manifesting 'the presence of the absence', the break, 'snatching away from the routine identity of the everyday'. Thus with modernity, aesthetic experience, which formerly was only a support leading to the sacred, a means, becomes an end in itself – art for art's sake.

The survival of religious experience is a phenomenon which for Gauchet only concerns the individual (300). The three structures of experience formerly understood as religious experience can only exist in the register of being, affecting or being affected by history, by society and by the institutions only in an accidental way; consequently what was religious experience and what one would give another name to today is a basic anthropological structure, an *a priori* scheme, constituting itself outside history. Religious experience 'as a condition of transhistorical possibility' on which religion as an institution has found a basis, can very well dispense with established religion. To understand this 'basis', this anthropological structure, there is no need to go through an examination of religion.

III. Summary and questions

Gauchet speaks of a move from the social function of religion to a subjective function of religious experience. In reality this is not a move, since religion as a system, as institution and discourse, completely disappears with the abolition of its social function. What from now on assumes a subjective function is not religion as an institution but individual experience of a religious order that one could equally term aesthetic experience, experience of the self, etc. If religious experience as a scheme structuring human beings can function 'in a void', without content, it is because it has a 'solipsist', immediate, pre-reflective nature. The maintaining of religious experience within modernity constitutes an aporia which can be summed up around two basic questions: the unilateral attachment of religious experience to aesthetic rationality, and the solipsist character of religious experience.

The reduction of religious experience to aesthetic rationality
Once religion is definitively reduced to the private sphere, only the sphere of subjective experience can be the basis for religious experiences as aesthetic experiences. The aestheticizing of religious experience restricts it to being mediated solely through aesthetic reality, and the consequence of that is that its only mode of epistemological validation will be the subjective 'sense effect' that it produces on the subject. But if this is true, do we have to conclude that the theoretical and practical dimensions of religion, which are expressed in dogmatic and ethical discourse, must be conceived of equally as being mediated solely by aesthetic rationality?

The solipsist character of religious experience
Marcel Gauchet has given us a perfect illustration of the epistemological background to the subjective function of religious experience. Religious experience was defined explicitly by its pre-reflective and non-discursive character of immediacy, of rising out of being; religious experience is thus conceived of in accordance with the criteria of the Romantic pre-hermeneutic view of expressive experience; so experience is the anterior 'foundation' to any linguistic and cultural expression. It is an *a priori*, a historical and pre-linguistic scheme which ignores all social mediation.[7] This model of experience causes more difficulties than it resolves by thinking that the nature of religious discourse is other than expressionist, i.e. dogmatic and practical discourse. To suppose that the latter is governed only by cognitive or moral rationalities, and cut off from religious experience, would pose as much of a dilemma as to think of it as strictly organized only by aesthetic rationality. A relationship between experience and discourse, if it is of an expressive and unilateral order – experience being first and its expression second – would consequently subject the whole dimension of discourse to aesthetic rationality, to sentiment, to the

irrationality of immediacy. As for religion, it would only be seen as the enemy of the experience of a faith – according to an all-too-familiar scheme within which only faith is authentic. Religion, marred by sociality, is thus derived and secondary, and at best could relate only to the direct expression of the experience of faith.

The logic of modernity that we have followed with the thoughts of Habermas and Gauchet thus necessarily seems to relegate religious experience, religion, religious language and theological discourse either to oblivion or to irrationalism. So is religion conceived of as being 'the Other of Reason', on which some post-modern theologians hope to found a new atheology? To escape the impasses of modernity, theology must more than ever investigate itself and its epistemological foundations as *fides quaerens intellectum*, on the basis of a renewed concept of religious experience and rationality.[8]

Translated by John Bowden

Notes

1. Jürgen Habermas, *La technique et la science comme 'ideologie'*, Paris 1973, 33.
2. Jürgen Habermas, *Theory of Communicative Action*, Vol. 2, Oxford 1988, 88.
3. Jean-Louis Schlegel, 'Réconcilier la modernité avec elle-même', *Esprit* 10, 1987, 119 (my italics).
4. Marcel Gauchet, *Le désenchantement du monde*, Paris 1985.
5. Gauchet mentions several of these ways, including the aesthetic sense and the 'modalities of the practice of the self'. Should we see here a reference to Michel Foucault's last work?
6. Gauchet is referring to Rudolf Otto's Book *The Idea of the Holy*, London 1923.
7. For a hermeneutical analysis of religious experience see Edward Schillebeeckx, *Church. The Human Story of God*, London and New York 1990.
8. I have undertaken this work in my doctoral thesis *Pour une théorie rationnelle de l'herméneutique en théologie*, Paris, Université de Paris-Sorbonne et Institut Catholique de Paris, June 1991.

III · The Crisis of Modernity and the Church's Attitudes

What is Christian about Europe?
Rudolf von Thadden

I am glad that my topic is not 'How Christian is Europe?' Had it been, I would have had to take the risky course of a quantitative analysis of the extent of the Christian penetration of Europe, which can presumably be measured. I would have had to investigate the extent of the (so-called) 'Christianization' of spheres of life, and consider how far the conduct of individuals or societies is still or no longer 'Christian'. And very soon I would probably have found myself caught up in the chorus of nostalgic complaints that Europe is unfortunately so 'de-Christianized' that it runs the risk of losing itself. There I would prefer to follow Martin Luther, who, in his work 'Temporal Authority: To What Extent Should it be Obeyed', warned against an excessive estimate of the possibilities of Christianization and soberly concluded: 'I am satisfied to point out that it is not impossible for a prince to be a Christian, although it is a rare thing and beset with difficulties.'[1]

However, my question is not 'How Christian is Europe?' but 'What is Christian about Europe?' So we shall be looking not at the extent of Christianity but at its specific features in Europe. What traces, one might also ask, has Christianity left behind in the European world? What forms of our life can be said to have been determined by Christianity?

To find an answer to these questions we should leave aside the discussion fronts of the nineteenth century and put behind us the dispute between believing Christians and non-believing atheists about whether the effects of Christian faith are healthy or pernicious. Rather, we should try to look at Europe, our world shaped by Christianity, and see with non-European eyes what we take for granted there. Then the issue becomes not so much one of belief and unbelief as of what forces in European culture made possible that powerful technological, economic and scientific development which today is the basis for the predominance of the 'West'. Not Christianity as a 'religion of redemption', as people would have said earlier, but Christian faith as a possible driving force in that breathtaking process of modernization which has changed our world more in a few generations than in the previous twenty centuries; which makes people from non-European cultures look at Europe and among other things investigate its Christian components.

It is doubtless the Islamic world which at present is moved most strongly by such considerations. Whether in the sphere of the Gulf War and the fights between Sadam Hussein and the fundamentalist Shi'ites, or in the field of conflict in France between North African immigrants and indigenous people anxious about their identity, everywhere particular phenomena of a superiority of Western European forms of civilization are emerging and prompting questions about their basic causes. Are non-European cultures less in a position to achieve technological and scientific progress because of their approach? Are there merely fortuitous reasons, conditioned by circumstances, which prevent the Islamic world from going along with Europe and the West?

In more recent Arab discussion a phenomenon is emphasized in this connection which is also being noted increasingly in sociological research: that of intellectual and cultural processes for coping with social change. There is a change in social structures wherever the process of industrialization takes place. But do people also have the power to assimilate this culturally and cope with it without damaging their own lives? This is the anxious question which concerns, for example, the Islamic scholar Bassam Tibi, who comes from Syria, and who asserts in a recent investigation that 'Muslims must react to changed situations with a cultural system which in their own self-understanding can be brought to completion and is unchangeable.'[2]

So can we say – and here I would make the question more pointed in the context of our discussion – that as a religion Islam is too static, too little capable of development, to do justice to the challenges of our world, caught up as it is in permanent change? And conversely, can one really assert with a good conscience that Christianity and the cultural world bound up with it has more internal forces for renewal than Islam, and reacts more flexibly to social change? Anyone who considers the Catholic moral teaching of our days and, for example, has read the Pope's remarks on contraception and birth control on the occasion of his recent visit to Poland, will have been critical here and warn against self-righteous Christian declarations.

'Christian' Europe is viewed from yet another perspective in Indian culture, shaped by Hinduism. Here it is less the conduct of Europeans towards the modern world which provokes critical questions or even anxieties, than an element of the ethical orientation of life: the excessive materialism of people who are rooted in European, Western culture. After a return from one of his numerous trips to Europe, the Indian scholar Sundar Singh wrote with great disappointment: 'One day I was sitting on a river bank in the Himalayas. I took a beautiful, round, hard stone out of the water and shattered it. The inside was quite dry. This stone had lain in the water for a long time, but the water had not penetrated the stone. That is what it is like with people in Europe: for centuries they have had Christianity flowing around them; they are utterly immersed in its blessings; they live in Christianity, but Christianity has not penetrated them and does not live in them. The fault does not lie with Christianity but with the hardness of hearts. Materialism and intellectualism have made hearts hard.'[3]

So Europe is seen as a place of the futility and superficiality of Christian faith, an exhausted soil which produces no fruit for life. Here Christianity loses its spiritual power because Europe seeks the kingdom of God in externals and means to build it by civilization and a general renewal of the world. For Gandhi, our part of the world was 'Christian only in name'. Here traces of the message of Jesus get lost in ideas of a supposedly Christian culture which thinks more of shaping world conditions externally than of the inner renewal of human beings.

Think of how many people in Europe are convinced that Christian culture lies at the heart of the identity of our continent! How many Christians, not least, answer the question 'What is Christian about Europe?' by referring to those well-worn words 'Christian culture', though without being able to indicate precisely what they mean! In some connections they even go so far as to talk of the supposedly 'Christian soul' of Europe, which has to be preserved in the face of all threats.

But let us also not take this criticism too lightly. If Herr Mazowiecki was invited to Germany from Warsaw, he would certainly not hesitate to speak of the values of Polish culture with its Christian stamp, which made many citizens of his country able to stand firm over the decades of first National Socialist and then Communist tyranny. In his view the 'Christian culture' of Poland would be the interplay of all forms of spirit and life which determine human behaviour in the confusions of today's world, weary of revolution, and are able to offer some orientation.

It is more than understandable that in this context two 'values' above all are emphasized, the violation of which was the order of the day in the systems of domination fashioned by Hitler and Stalin: those of human rights and personal freedom. Freedom and human rights: those were the slogans which formed around resistance to totalitarian rule; those were the concepts which gave people new hope – despite all the differences in their situations.

However, what is noticeable when these values are conjured up is not the fact as such, the way in which they are identified with Christianity as a matter of course. It occurs to hardly anyone that over important periods of our European history freedom and human rights were demanded not *with*, but *in the face of*, the Christian churches. When two hundred years ago, at the time of the French revolution, these terms were propagated as battle slogans, those who used them received no support from the churches and their dignitaries, but rather incurred hostility. In 1789 there was no assent either from the Catholic bishops or from the Lutheran prelates and court preachers to the demand for freedom and human rights.

So is what many people today feel to be Christian about European culture not so Christian at all? In France 150 years ago there was a discussion on this very question, a discussion which was little known in Germany, though it concerns us as much as the French. On the one side there was the spiritual father of modern European racism, Arthur de Gobineau, who with his *Essay on the Inequality of the Human Races* was later to influence the confused notions of the Nazis. On the other side was the great political thinker Alexis de Tocqueville, who with his secular work *On Democracy in America* held up to Europeans the mirror of their irreversible course towards the equality of civil rights. Tocqueville raised the question what had changed with the rise of Christianity in Europe, and came to the conclusion that not least modern democracy also drew on the renewing forces of Christian faith. By contrast, Gobineau saw Christianity as neither a pioneering innovation nor a herald of the modern world, and regarded the way in which this world had become the focus of attention since the Enlightenment as the real revolution of our age. For Tocqueville, even a modern, democratic and secularized Europe had to refer to forms of the Christian image of man; without them, in the long term it would fall victim to moral decline. By contrast, for Gobineau a Europe without Christianity was not only conceivable but in some circumstances even desirable, because it would be more prepared to take developments as given (by nature) and does not make excessive demands on people.[4]

So what was the influence of Christianity on European history? Did it encourage the modern forces of freedom or cause anxiety about them? Did it help or hinder the European peoples, on their way into the modern world of pluralistic democracy, to cope with the new demands? Anyone who reads the most recent church statements, above all from the Catholic side, gets the impression that here the balance sheet is made out to be predominantly positive. Thus when the Pope addressed the Council of Europe in Strasbourg on 8 October 1988, he said: 'The biblical view of man allowed Europeans to develop a great idea of the dignity of human beings as persons; this is an essential value even for those who have no religious faith.' And he went on to say in connection with the frontiers of Europe: 'Down the centuries Europe has played a significant role in other parts of the world. It must be conceded that Europe did not always give of its best in its encounter with the other civilizations, but no one can doubt that in a happy way it allowed them to share in many values which it had brought to maturity over a long period.'[5]

So here we have a picture of a Europe shaped by Christianity, in which the positive features predominate. Granted, it is conceded that this Europe 'did not always give of its best', above all in its encounter with other civilizations or cultures, but on the whole there is no doubt here that European history is more one of blessing than of guilt, and that in particular the contribution of Christianity has more light than shade. No words about the threat to cultures outside Europe from European colonialism, no words about the persecution of those with other views in the process of the rise of the modern world, and – above all – not a word about the scourge of European antisemitism, which is not just accidentally and incidentally part of the history of Christian Europe. According to this speech by the Pope, Europe does not need to overcome the past in order to gain the future.

But from the Protestant side, too, statements on the theme of Europe are no more satisfactory. Here the sense of a Christian Europe is less marked, and so there are virtually no viable statements about what Europe is or should be. There is no Protestant concept of Europe. As a rule Europe is regarded only as an economic community or a political alliance of states with kindred interests in which Christians have to prove themselves in loyal single combat. For the Protestant church in Germany, the local state churches are still the most important place of service and commitment. And beyond the national framework, for those in the Evangelical Church of Germany there is only the ecumenical movement and the World Council of Churches to direct attention to worldwide Christianity. There is hardly anything worth considering between Germany and the world.[6]

This is not at all good, and fails to do justice to reality. A century ago, in the time of domination by nation states, the lack of viable conceptions of Europe might still be passed over, but today, at a time when a concrete political European community has come into being, this is very worrying. For Europe is taking shape before our eyes without a satisfactory contribution from responsible Christians. If I relate my topic 'What is Christian about Europe?' to the present and narrow it down to the question 'What is Christian about Europe *today*?', I stumble and stammer. On the one hand there is Western Europe, which is developing almost exclusively in accordance with categories of increased economic profitability and has no voice at times of political crisis like the weeks of the Gulf War. And on the other side there is Eastern Europe which, after the collapse of the Communist regime, is hovering between dreams of capitalistic miracle worlds and lapses into nationalistic unilateralism. In the first instance Christianity is at best an ideological extra, useful for papering over the cracks in the brickwork of a policy orientated on power and profit. In the other, as a substratum of historical myths hostile to modernity, it fills the vacuum of political and moral formative power left behind by decades of Communist rule. In both cases, the power of a Christian faith which is at the same time both critical and renewing can only be traced fleetingly.

But the process of European union is going forward and will not wait until we present ecumenically agreed plans from a Christian perspective. So I want to present eight theses on the current question of what Europe could be today from a Protestant perspective.

Thesis 1

Europe is not a Christian stockade but a historically shaped place of Christian testimony in a world which is determined equally by the forces of faith and the forces of doubt. The Europe in which we live today is shaped not only by the traditions of the Christian churches but also by the impulses of the Enlightenment and its critique of tradition. So it must take shape in dialogue and – possibly also – conflict between Christian faith and the secularized world; it cannot allow a lapse either into Christian fundamentalism or self-satisfied rationalism. Only a combination of faith related to reality and tolerance of those with other views can give a power of conviction to human life in the challenges of the present.

Thesis 2

Europe is not a closed cultural sphere but a place in world politics where other cultures can be considered and accepted. A Europe which shuts out people with a different cultural formation forfeits its future and alienates itself from itself.

This is true today more than ever. For the European union of our days is taking place at a time when the nations of Europe hardly exist any longer as monocultural units. Among us there is hardly a city in which extensive ethnic minorities do not live – for the most part from cultures outside Europe. Algerians in France and Turks in Germany remind us that Europe's identity can only be open and many-sided. Christians should not find it hard to affirm this.

Thesis 3

Europe is not only an economic sphere but also a community of people, of citizens. Important though the constantly ongoing interweaving of economic interests may be for the process of European union, it must not become independent and develop in an uncontrolled luxuriance. The Europe of industrialists and businessmen remains responsible to the Europe of citizens.

So the sphere of competence of the European parliament must be extended and its authority strengthened. Furthermore, forms of the civil rights movement must develop further in Europe so that human contact is not lost in the increasingly wide spheres of trade. European union makes democratic collaboration more important than ever.

Thesis 4

Europe is not only a sphere of responsibility for politicians but also for the Christian churches. Called to bear witness to and serve humanity, they have to take account of the new social structures which have grown up in Europe and work within them. That means that the churches must be ready to examine their own structures critically to see whether they live up to the new demands. In the long run it cannot be satisfactory for a European parliament only to have conversation partners with credentials from national churches in the Protestant sphere, while the episcopal conferences dominate the Catholic world. With the growing tasks facing European decision-making bodies, it is time to form European synods which articulate and responsibly give shape to the contribution of Christians to the social and cultural building up of Europe. Mere conferences of church dignitaries are not enough here.

Thesis 5

Europe as a challenge for the churches: that is not just a matter of the contribution of Christians to the building up of new European structures but also a question about the significance of Europe for the life of the churches. So it is more than doubtful whether we can do justice to it by keeping the old confessional divisions while the growing together of Europe is demolishing or blurring boundaries. Is it not time that we learned to relativize historically formations which have grown up in church history as we do those which have grown up in state history, and stop taking confessions more seriously than nations? How much unrest we could spare ourselves if, for example, today in Eastern Europe the confessional boundaries between Roman Catholic and Greek Orthodox churches were treated as what they are: as frontiers which have grown up in history between the Polish and the Russian-Ukrainian spheres of influence! The issue here is not primarily that of differences between theological views but above all of different types of piety which have been shaped in different ways and which find their expression in particular modes of behaviour and forms of cultural life. Let us de-dogmatize church history.

Thesis 6

Europe is not a mere extrapolation of existing traditions but a chance of renewal. Just as the Europe of the patriots can become a Europe of the citizens, so the Europe of the official churches can and should develop into a Europe in which local communities are more lively and communicate more with one another. What people expect from Christians in the future is not the proclamation of authoritative doctrinal opinions but communicative language and practical solidarity with those in need of help and at their wits' end in the often merciless process of the unification of Europe. For that we need horizontal rather than vertical structures, forums which make an exchange of experiences possible rather than pulpits which are made for sermons; readiness for human participation rather than paternalistic practices. In a word, it would do us good if we again accepted more of the impulses of the lay movement which shaped the Kirchentag in the years of the new beginning after the war and which could still be effective today. Europe offers much scope for forces ready for renewal.

Thesis 7

Despite a recognition of all that has been achieved so far, Europe is more than the European community of the twelve states of Brussels. Though we have good reason to maintain the community of Western Europe and deepen it, we must open the doors to Eastern Europe and develop Europe beyond the frontiers of the European Community. But we will be able to do this only if we do not just construct defence policies but also structures which create peace, which encourage the practice of peaceful co-existence even among people and communities shaped in different ways. Peace is more than disarmament; to be secured it also requires a humanization of society and living conditions. And for that an expanded Europe with its related cultural foundations offers a hopeful basis. As Christians we all have occasion to collaborate in the work.

Thesis 8

Europe is more than the legacy of its successes, elevating though it may be to keep remembering them. Down the centuries there has always been a history of European failure, indeed suffering, which has shaped human consciousness. Poor people begged for entry at the gates of cities, fugitives for reasons of faith hoped for acceptance in neighbouring countries, political emigrants sought protection beyond their own frontiers. What would Europe be without the history of its persecutions, but also without the experiences of a solidarity it has been given? In exile, those who had been persecuted in Hitler's Reich experienced what European community could mean – long before there was such a community in the present economic and political sense. In this sense the Europe that needs to be built up will have to develop a collective memory not only of its political and cultural achievements but also of its frequent historical failures. For this collective memory makes it possible to share in the bearing of burdens which have come down to us from our history. Europe has to prove itself as a community of solidarity.[7]

Translated by John Bowden

Notes

1. Martin Luther, 'Temporal Authority: To What Extent Should it be Obeyed', in *Martin Luther's Basic Theological Writings*, ed. T. F. Lull, Minneapolis 1989, 695.

2. Bassam Tibi, *Der Islam und das Problem der kulturellen Bewältigung sozialen Wandels*, Frankfurt am Main 1985, 242.

3. Sundar Singh, quoted from Friedrich Heiler, *Sadhu Sundar Singh. Ein Apostel des Ostens und Westens*, Munich 1924, 58f.

4. *Correspondence d'Alexis de Tocqueville et d'Arthur de Gobineau*, Volume IX of Oeuvres complètes de A. De Tocqueville, ed. J.-P. Mayer, Paris 1959, 45ff.

5. Quoted from the weekend German-language edition of *Osservatore Romano*, 18 November 1988. The first quotation comes from the Pope's greeting to the French state president, the second from his address to the Parliamentary Assembly of the Council of Europe in Strasbourg.

6. Cf. especially Reinhard Frieling, 'Europa und die Kirchen. Plädoyer für eine Europäische Evangelische Synode', in *Materialdienst des Konfessionskundlichen Instituts Bensheim* 3/1990, 47ff.

7. Cf. my 'Kulturelle Vielfalt und Bürgersinn im künftigen Europa', in Rudolf von Thadden, *Nicht Vaterland, nicht Fremde. Essays zu Geschichte und Gegenwart*, Munich 1989, 175ff.

The Debate about Modernity in the North Atlantic World and the Third World

Juan Carlos Scannone

The debate about modernity and post-modernity in Europe and North America has vital relevance for the Third World, where the need for modernization (in science and technology, politics and culture) clashes with the need for respect for justice and national identity.

I shall approach this subject by first explaining what I mean by modernity and outlining the main positions in the current North Atlantic debate on the subject. In the second part of this article I shall consider the issue from the point of view of the Third World, with special reference to Latin America. In this way I shall provide the basis for an answer to the questions raised.

I. The concept of modernity and the modernity debate

Modernity as a historico-cultural movement is defined by the four modern revolutions, not always simultaneous in their outbreak or course: the scientific, political, cultural and technical revolutions.[1]

The scientific revolution broke with the symbolic understanding of the world and began to regard it as self-regulating. Human beings were no longer the mediators of the world, but investigators of its laws and transformers of the world by their action. The political revolution broke with the main privileges of a society structured as a hierarchy of orders and replaced them with a functional concept of society and by representative democracy and its formal procedures. The cultural revolution consisted in the Enlightenment, defined by Kant as the adult state of humanity (reason and freedom), without the guardianship of external authorities. The technical revolution replaced agricultural and craft work and human-scale implements by industrial and post-industrial work, which increasingly abstracts from the human factor and replaces it by a techno-structure: this has been a continuous process from the beginning of manufacture, via steam engines and the industrial complex, to the new technologies based on informatics and robots.

The Enlightenment analysed the common features of these revolutions, namely (1) their base in critical and secular reason, (2) the self-reference both of reason itself (self-transparency) and human freedom (autonomy and self-realization) and of the world in its self-regulated totality and in the immanent complex differentiation of its sub-systems,[2] (3) formalism (mathematical description, the predominance of dialectic, functionalization, structuralism and informatization).

Modernity understood in these terms is in crisis. There is a more or less general consensus among the best qualified observers, not only about the fact of the crisis, but also that a particular way of understanding reason and subjectivity are no longer valid. After a first stage dominated by a purely analytic, formal, linear and instrumental rationality (eighteenth century), the nineteenth century saw the pre-eminence of the systematic form (whether dialectical or functionalist) of the same rationality, which became increasingly totalizing and even totalitarian. The final phase of the influence of this form came in the second half of the twentieth century, when this rationality reached its limits in all dimensions of society and culture.[3] The most radical evidence of this fact can probably be seen in science and the theory of science, where the idea of a unitary, total science has been abandoned, and with it the idea of absolute justification, grounding or verification. This was the end of the ideology of scientism.

The other most visible manifestation of the same crisis has been the failure of totalizing philosophical systems and the various types of totalitarian political systems, and the ideologies and utopias which sustained them. This led to a questioning of any absolutizing of reason, whether instrumental or dialectical. However, this crisis is making itself ever more evident in the experience of the limits of material development and progress once thought to be indefinite, now called in question by growing ecological and human deterioration. Accordingly philosophers have spoken of the 'end of the modern age' (Romano Guardini) and of the 'surpassing of the philosophy of subjectivity' (Heidegger), understood in terms of the ego (individual, transcendental or collective) and in terms of consciousness in its relation of position and domination *vis à vis* the other – and others – considered merely as objects.

Some analysts regard the crisis as affecting only cultural modernity or some of its aspects. Others see it only as the crisis of one way of understanding and living modernity and the modern revolutions, namely those mentioned in the previous paragraph, but insist that the project of modernity as such is still unfinished. Others again prefer to talk about post-modernity, though they interpret this in different ways, either as a radicalization of modernity or its abandonment, whether as a negative or a positive phenomenon. In other words, in this debate there are at least three different and opposing positions: (1) the neo-conservative, (2) the post-modern, (3) that of critical theory and communicative rationality.[4]

The neo-conservative position (for example, Daniel Bell) reaffirms the validity of functional rationality and capitalist logic, the motors of scientific-technological and techno-economic production. According to the neo-conservatives, these are the source of the advances achieved by modernity, based on values such as economic rationality, discipline, efficiency, postponement of immediate pleasure for the sake of future goals, etc. The crisis, they say, is caused by cultural modernity, both by its hypercritical and libertarian spirit and by an exaggerated (modern and post-modern) stress on aesthetics and expression. This shows itself in individualist experimentalism, in the search for immediate pleasure and in attempts to achieve self-realization and authenticity without rules.

However, the neo-conservative position does not see the structural links between the cultural phenomena it criticizes and the capitalist logic of the self-regulated and self-regulating market, which it accepts. It does not understand that the obvious consequence of this is a society which is individualistic, hedonistic and consumerist to a point at which it sinks into the practical nihilism of drug addiction. Moreover, the outright rejection of cultural modernity implies the danger of a return to an external and imposed system of rules and a fixed and ahistorical rationality, which has not assimilated all that is valid in the critical, autonomous and creative spirit typical of the Enlightenment. Even more, neo-conservatism sometimes goes so far as uncritically to proclaim 'the end of history' (Francis Fukuyama), in the sense of the end of ideologies, without making clear that assertion itself conceals the ideology of neo-liberalism.

Some conservative Christian positions today unfortunately play into the hands of the neo-liberals. They tend naively to accept late capitalist society while totally rejecting the Enlightenment, and fail to see the humanizing and the reductionist components in both.

After the failure of the unitary and totalizing systems and the great ideological meta-discourses which validated them, post-modernism gives a positive value to difference, pluralism, relativization, deconstruction, disagreement and difference (J.-F. Lyotard). It does this on the basis of the aesthetic experience of the incommensurability of styles, the mutual irreducibility of language games or life-forms, and the instant enjoyment of what simply happens. It is a nihilism, but a positive nihilism inspired by Nietzsche. Nietzsche's phrase, 'Dancing on the edge of the abyss',[5] is a good description of this attitude. We are on the edge of an abyss because the 'God of metaphysics' has died, and with him every attempt at transparent, absolute and total validation, but we dance at the prospect of the ethical and aesthetic liberation of new possibilities. This is not an abandonment of critical reason – which is a legacy from modernity – but it is a weak philosophical system (G. Vattimo), a plural and irreducibly heterogeneous rationality, ambiguous (without self-transparency), and with merely transversal connections, which do not converge at a centre and are not hierarchically ordered.

There are also Christian attempts to go 'beyond secular reason' (J. Milbank) and thus beyond modernity, without integrist nostalgias for pre-modernity, rather an attempt to advance towards an integral post-modernity.[6] For these thinkers, as for Heidegger, the essence of modernity is contained in desire for power and, ultimately, in a meta-discourse of violence. However, according to this interpretation, the nihilist post-modernists – more or less inspired by Nietzsche – although they criticize the great mythical and ideological accounts, also return, in their nihilism, to the originating myth of primordial violence. The only alternative to this, argue these Christians, the real post-modernism, is the Christian proto-account of gratuitous creation out of love and its ethical corollary based on a praxis marked by the primacy of peace and an ontology of difference, not understood dialectically in terms of opposition and negation (J. Derrida), nor even positively but conflictively (G. Deleuze), but in terms of a social relation of positive otherness, of difference in the communion of analogy and of gratuitous reciprocity.

Critical theory (J. Habermas, K.- O. Apel) insists that the modern project – as formulated by the Enlightenment – is still unfinished and has sufficient utopian reserves to be achieved. With Max Weber it accepts the differentiation and autonomous status of the different dimensions of society and culture as an important gain of modernity, but it rejects the dissolution of reason into ambiguity and opacity, and of its unity into mere difference. It argues that the plurality of language games and life forms is precisely where we have to rediscover the unity of reason between the mutually irreducible areas of instrumental rationality (science and technology), normative rationality (ethics and politics) and aesthetics.

After linguistic philosophy and the consequent abandonment of the philosophy of the ego and consciousness, this unity has to be sought in communicative action and reason (Habermas) and the (ideal and real) community of communication (Apel). For Habermas the ordinary language of the life-world provides the meta-language common to the different specialized languages, so that it is possible to rediscover 'in the medium of language a weak, transitory unity of reason'.[7] For Apel a transcendental language game takes place in and beyond the different empirical language games.[8]

In this way communicative reason makes it possible to counteract the 'colonization of the life-world' (Habermas) by economic systems (the market) and political and administrative systems (the bureaucracy), without abandoning either the modern differentiation of dimensions and languages or the unity, provisional and fallible though it may be, of reason. Every participant in conversation in every type of language shares the claim that what they say is valid.

This also gives us a new way of understanding the self-reference characteristic of modernity, no longer in the mode of the ego and consciousness, but in the mode of the community of communication and language and significant action, whose meaning is essentially social and public.

In my view, a deeper understanding of community, communication, language and communicative reason and action leads to a radical redefinition of the Enlightenment concept of self-reference. If we redefine self-reference in terms of community and communication, we find that the 'self' in question is revealed, lived and understood primarily in terms of the other (*autrui*), in a relationship of ethical otherness and transcendence (E. Lévinas). And, on the other hand, such a radicalization could lead to the abandonment of an understanding of communicative reason which is still too narrow, namely as primarily argumentative, discursive and formal (through the use of formal procedures for seeking consensus in Habermas, or through *a priori* transcendental forms, in Apel).

II. Modernity and modernization in the Third World

The debate about modernity has its special, and more conflictive, features in the Third World because it reaches here from outside. The history of reason as it began in Greece is particular to the so-called West, but nevertheless the Third World is in a headlong process of modernization.

Experience has shown that modern science and technology, when not considered in themselves but in their social and cultural impact, are not neutral instruments which can adapt to cultures without changing them profoundly. Science and technology have their own socio-cultural logic in the sense that they imply a break with the mythical conception of the world. Paul Ricoeur has drawn attention to the threat and challenge represented by modern universal civilization for national cultures and their ethico-mythical nuclei.[9] And, among others, J. Ladrière has studied the transfer of attitudes and perspectives from science and technology to other areas of culture such as ethics or aesthetics, with the resulting challenge to cultures.[10]

On top of all this is the fact that cultural transformation takes place in a historical process factually characterized by conflict, imperialism, oppression and dependence. In this way modernity is used as an ideology, whether as a pretext and instrument of domination or as a weapon and goal of a counter-attack. This aspect becomes more serious if we consider the desire for power as essential to the *ethos* of modernity, or at least to the form of modernity which has predominated until now and has gone into crisis. This has given rise to the parallel drawn between the 'I conquer' of colonialism (E. Dussel) and the modern *ego cogito* and 'I work', inasmuch as they embody a relation of subject-object domination. The foreign debt, the adjustment measures imposed by financial institutions, the deterioration of the terms of trade, and so on, are in this view current versions of imperialism, with the consequent widening of the gulf between rich and poor, superdeveloped and underdeveloped.

In fact, it was not only the market or particular technological (e.g. military) advances, but also other modern values such as science and technology themselves, democracy or even the Enlightenment, which were and are used as ideological instruments to dominate, oppress or marginalize the Third World. In Latin America the contrast 'civilization or barbarism' became famous as a summary of the alienating contempt for our own cultures.

In the Third World the debate, almost from the beginning, has taken the form of a battle between naive acceptance and systematic rejection of everything modern. In between there are those who want to separate the eager acceptance of modern (scientific, technological, economic and legal) instruments from the cultural transformation they imply. Very often there is also the silent cultural resistance of the people.

In the face of the threat to national identity, there are generally two nationalist strategies, the fundamentalist and the revolutionary. Both, appealing to tradition, reinterpret it, recreate it and sometimes invent it, with a tendency to convert it into an ideology opposed to modernity, which is also interpreted as an ideology. Fundamentalism ideologizes tradition to make it a weapon for the rejection of what is alien and foreign; often it finds resources in an ahistorical conception of religion itself (as is happening with Islamic fundamentalism). The revolutionary position, in contrast, tries to bring the old culture to modernity. For this purpose it also ideologizes both, absorbing them into the real North-South conflict and to the necessary struggle against structures of oppression. This means an attempt to achieve modernity in equality, without radically transforming either the old culture or the model of Western modernity which is the goal.

The current North Atlantic debate about modernity – which, with different protagonists but analogous forms – has also been taking place in the Third World – may help to clarify phenomena, practices and proposals which appear in the Third World debate. The neo-conservative position is reproduced in its entirety in both environments, and the same critique applies, except that, in view of the structural injustice generated by capitalist class society and its international influence, the questioning to which it is subjected by the Third World is even more radical.

Post-modernism, with its critique of logocentrism and the totalitarianism of reason, and its stress on plurality and difference, enables the Third World to free itself from Eurocentrism or any centrism which tends to oppress, and to recognize its own difference and sapiential rationality within plural rationality. In addition, the value attached to the ludic and aesthetic dimension, the critique of any forced unification, respect for dissent, regard for ambiguity, appreciation of lateral connections, etc. are connected with respect for the irreducible otherness of peoples and their cultural language games. They coincide with the cultural values of the Third World and its desire to liberate its own potential imaginatively and creatively. However, on the other hand, ambiguity, plurality and nihilistic deconstruction threaten capacity for communal initiatives characteristic of the common people, their capacity for hope and collective action, and the ethico-mythical roots of their cultures.

Communicative reason, for its part, appears to respond to the sense of community, solidarity, reciprocity and gratuitousness typical of many of the threatened cultures, reconciling it with the modern differentiation of cultural environments in the plural and non-prescriptive unity of reason. This is the approach of its critique of the colonization of the life-world by modern sub-systems, to accept them but transform them.

Thus, in my view, as I have already implied, reason has to be understood in a broader and more radical way than critical theory does, and sapiential and symbolic rationality included. The return to this rationality takes place in a sort of 'secondary naivety' (Ricoeur), which has come through critical theory and the differentiation of autonomous dimensions of action. Just as the understanding of the ego is relocated in terms of the 'we' (the communicating community), so scientific rationality has to be relocated in terms of a 'secondary' sapiential rationality, and analytic, transcendental and/or dialectical concepts in terms of symbols understood anew post-critically. For this to happen it is essential to recreate the symbolic space of cultures which assimilate modernity, being transformed and transforming it.

Modernization seems not only necessary but also inevitable for the Third World, but everything depends on the process. Earlier I criticized alienating modernizing attitudes which take no account of their own past or ideologize it. A. Jeannière says that the 'transition to modernity' does not mean 'erasing the past in order to end in the monochrome world of a universalized Western culture. It simply means, for each individual, accepting their past in such a way that traditions are neither a block nor an idea, but a starting point for a future as different from others as any cultural past.'[11] Japan could provide an example.

This is not just an idealistic proposal; there are phenomena emerging which need to be detected and evaluated. The history of Latin America includes not only various attempts at modernization which were on the whole unsuccessful (positivist, populist, developmentalist, etc.), but also a number of successful 'vital syntheses' between traditional culture and modern values (emancipation, constitutional rule, public education, universal suffrage, social rights, industrialization, trade union rights, etc.). In addition, there is talk of an 'emerging modernity' among the Latin American poor (Clodovis Boff).[12] A new synthesis between the people's sapiential culture and modernity is taking place among the poor, transforming both from within. I am talking about the so-called 'base neo-communitarianism'.[13] This shows itself in the various cultural spheres: in religion with the ecclesial base communities, Bible study groups and prayer groups, in the social sphere with free popular organizations of various types and multi-sectoral movements, in economic activity in the popular economy of solidarity (workers' businesses, co-operatives, communal workshops),[14] in culture with 'modern' popular initiatives such as local radio stations. What is new about this is the combination of traditional values (community, solidarity, gratuitousness, the sapiential and religious sense) with modern elements: historical praxis, rationality, efficiency; efficient and participatory economic structures in which the 'C' factor (community) develops a new logic different from that of the market and the state. Other modern components are political pluralism, functional leadership, new modes of exercising authority and of organization based on participation and solidarity. In the religious sphere there is renewal of popular piety through contact with the written word of God and with social and political awareness and action.

These are examples of ways in which the social and cultural creativity of the ordinary people of Latin America and the modern élites which emerge out of them or ally themselves with them seem to be moving in the direction of a new cultural synthesis. I think that something similar is taking place in other parts of the Third World.

The vital synthesis which seems to be forming in Latin America between modernity from outside and an emerging internal popular culture is a distinctive practical response to the current debate about modernity.

Translated by Francis McDonagh

Notes

1. Cf. A. Jeannière, 'Qu'est-ce la modernité?', *Études* 373, 1990, 499–510.
2. On self-reference, cf. J. Habermas, *Der philosophische Diskurs de Moderne*, Frankfurt 1985.
3. On the different stages of modern society, cf. P. Hünerman, 'Technische Gesellschaft und Kirche', *Theologische Quartalschrift* 163, 1983, 284–303.
4. Cf. J. Habermas, *Kleine politische Schriften* I–IV, Frankfurt 1981, 462–4.
5. *An den Abgründen tanzen*: cf. F. Nietzsche, *Die fröhliche Wissenschaft*, Nietzsche, *Werke. Kritische Gesamtausgabe* V–2, Berlin & New York 1973, 265.
6. E.g. J. Milbank, *Theology and Social Theory. Beyond Secular Reason*, Oxford 1990. See the excellent commentary by H. Lima Vaz, 'Além da Modernidade', *Síntese Nova Fase* 18, 1991, 241–54.
7. Cf. J. Habermas, *Nachmetaphysisches Denken*, Frankfurt 1988, 155.
8. Cf. K.– O. Apel, *Transformation der Philosophie* II, Frankfurt 1976, 245–63.
9. Cf. P. Ricoeur, 'Civilisation universelle et cultures nationales', *Histoire et variété*, Paris 1964, 286–300.
10. Cf. J. Ladrière, *Les enjeux de la rationalité. Le défi de la science et de la technologie aux cultures*, Paris 1977.
11. Cf. A. Jeannière, *Les fins du monde*, Paris 1987, 130.
12. C. Boff, 'Para onde irá a Igreja na América Latina?', *Revista Eclesiástica Brasileira* 50, 1990, 282. See also P. Trigo, 'Evangelización del cristianismo en los barrios de América Latina', *Revista Latinoamericano de Teología*, 6 1989, 89–113; J. Comblin, 'Evangelización y cultura. La cultura de los pobres', *Pastoral Popular* 195, 1989, supplement.
13. Cf. D. García Delgado, 'Las contradicciones culturales de los proyectos de modernización en los 80', *Le Monde diplomatique* (Latin American edition) 27–28, 1989, 15–18. See also my article, 'Nueva modernidad advenience y cultura emergente en América Latina. Reflexiones filosóficas y teológico-pastorales', *Stromata* 47, 1991, 145–92.
14. See L. Razeto's books, esp. *Economía popular de solidaridad y mercado democrático*, 3 vols., Santiago de Chile 1984–88.

The Attitude of the Church to the Modern World at and after Vatican II

Giovanni Turbanti

The attitude of the church at the Second Vatican Council to the modern world come of age corresponds in the first place to the transition from the interpretation of modernity as an ideological category, as it had been in the anti-modernist tradition, to a consideration of it as a strictly historical phenomenon. This transition was already indicated in a precise way in the intentions of John XXIII when he decided to convene a council, taking into account the particular situation of the modern world and remembering that human history had reached a crucial point in its course: '"The church today is witnessing a crisis in society," he wrote in the encyclical *Humanae salutis* with which he gave notice of the Council. "Whereas humanity is on the threshold of a new age, the church is faced with tasks of great seriousness and complexity, as in the most tragic eras of its history.""[1] The modernity which characterized this crucial point in history was an ambiguous category, because on the one hand it represented the positive development of human potential, but on the other hand it ended up conciding with the contradictions of which the society of the time was a victim. At any rate it was part of human history, and was a specific characteristic of a moment in its development. In the speech which opened the Council, prepared with deep reflection and meditation during August and September 1962, John XXIII said that the church would have to remain faithful to the 'heritage of truth received from the fathers', but at the same time would have to 'take account of the present, the new conditions and forms of life introduced into the modern world' which had opened up new ways for the apostolate. So the conciliar *magisterium* would have to be characterized as 'pre-eminently pastoral', and would have to seek to offer to people of today a new formulation of the deposit of faith. As he said, 'it is necessary for this certain and immutable doctrine, which must be faithfully respected, to be deepened and presented in a way which meets the demands of our time'.[2]

This pastoral choice, accepted by the fathers of the Council during the first session, represents the turning point in the attitude of the church to the modern world. In fact it corresponded to the forthright rejection of the doctrinal schemes developed by Cardinal Ottaviani's Preparatory Theological Commission and of the explicitly anti-modern positions which these schemes expressed. The Commission had worked in strict secrecy during the preparatory period to give a clear and unequivocal definition of all the doctrinal problems which had been the object of erroneous treatments in the preceding years. Although there would be no lack of discussion about them, in the end the schemes prepared for the Council gave the clear impression of being a dogged defence of the heavy weight of traditional doctrine against the threat from modern errors. The antimodernist perspective appeared not only in the scheme *De deposito Fidei pure custodiendo*, but also, significantly, in the chapter of *De Ecclesia* on the relationshp between the civil power and the religious power, where it was argued that the civil authority had a duty to safeguard religious freedom, but in favour of that institution which possessed the privilege of the truth, i.e. the Catholic church.[3] Here was the reaffirmation of an interpretative scheme of the relationships between the church and civil society which had grown up in the sphere of Catholic intransigence during the previous century, where an effective authority even over the civil order throughout 'Christendom' was attributed to the spiritual power of the Roman Pontiff. Here modernity was the old ideological cipher, representing all that opposed the tradition of Christian order. On the other hand, this perspective did not exclude the need which arose in the work of the other preparatory commissions for a renewal of certain aspects of church life and ecclesiastical discipline and a preoccupation with adapting ecclesial structures to the modern world. However, this did not correspond to the real significance of the *aggiornamento* proposed by John XXIII.

The 'dialogue' with the modern world according to Vatican II

At the Council, the level of confrontation with modernity was deeper. The 'pastoral approach' wanted by John XXIII brought into play the relationship between doctrine and the historical situation of modern society. It was not just a question of adapting the life of the church to modern conditions, but of a global rethinking of its very nature in the face of sociological and cultural realities towards which there was a concern no longer to be closed. This confrontation became the specific theme of some individual schemata, but in fact it had a profound effect on the discussions of the most important problems facing the Council. For example, it can be argued that in the redefinition of the church as the people of God there were reflections, on the one hand on the legal principle of individual equality, and on the other on the awareness of the greater degree of individual responsibility which the faithful had to bear in a secularized society. Thus in the difficult discussion on episcopal collegiality there was no lack of reference to modern parliamentary institutions, and the diversity of particular national situations was taken into account.

Quite soon there began to be talk at the Council of the need for the church to enter into dialogue with the world. The message approved by the fathers during the first days of their gathering in Rome also expressed this need. 'Dialogue' in some ways became the conciliar paradigm of the attitude of the church towards the modern world. But this soon proved to be too generic and imprecise a concept to cover quite diverse positions and attitudes within the church.

In the Commission for the Apostolate of the Laity the personalistic reading of Maritain found its most complete expression. From the 1930s onwards this reading had inspired many lay organizations for whom Maritain's reflections on the relative autonomy of temporal realities and the need for a civil commitment with a Christian inspiration had represented a way of getting through the straits of anti-modernism and becoming organically involved in the structures of society and the modern economy. However, despite the commitment of the Commission and the Pope's well-known sympathy for the French philosopher, Maritain's approach was not that chosen by the Council. Maritain's influence certainly made itself felt in the reflections on personalistic themes which appear in the doctrinal part of scheme XIII; however, the very nature of the 'pastoral approach' indicated by John XXIII in the opening speech to the Council, and then above all the teaching in *Pacem in terris*, represented a clear advance on the position proposed by Maritain in that they affirmed the existence of prophetic and gospel values also outside the project of the 'new Christianity' which he proposed.

It was in the group of the 'church of the poor' that the petitions most relevant to a new attitude of the church towards the world developed. However, this never succeeded in having any deep effect on the work of the Council, because although the problems which it raised were generally recognized to be fundamental, they were never focussed with sufficiently precise analyses, and the petitions put forward were often misunderstood as simple voluntarism. The Council faced the problem of poverty and underdevelopment by recognizing its great seriousness in the modern world, but the preferential option for the poor proposed by the group was not received with the centrality that it demanded.[4]

The scheme on The Church in the Modern World set out to offer a theological interpretation of earthly realities and to indicate how universally recognized moral principles could be translated into concrete attitudes. The Mixed Commission (Doctrine and for the Apostolate of the Laity) charged with its redaction wanted to get beyond the hypothesis of a general theology of 'earthly realities' which would have had to speak of the current situation in the light of theology. Following the indication given by John XXIII that 'signs of the times' were a theological key for interpreting the temporal realities of the modern world, the Commission started from the most general human values, which were a sign and work of the divine action. The basic hypothesis was that the most genuine expressions of modern culture and the highest values expressed by the modern civil conscience in fact represented manifestations of the divine grace operating in society. This thus followed the course already suggested in previous decades by the reflections of Fr Chenu on the economy of the incarnation: the 'signs of the times' pointed to history as a true theological subject, a place of a continual incarnation and a manifestation of grace; not a conceptual place but a concrete place, grasped in its dynamic and also its modernity. However, many fathers noted the risk that in the name of an exasperated quest for dialogue the church might have renounced the originality and the radical nature of its proclamation of the gospel and thus would have lost all credentials for speaking out. But the greatest weakness of the scheme became evident above all in the face of those situations in which the church was involved along with political and economic interests and which belied much of what the scheme wanted to affirm. This forced the commission to a laborious quest for mediation and balance in the text.[5]

The attitude of dialogue with the modern world encountered a decisive moment of testing in the discussion on religious freedom. Here there was an explicit contradiction between on the one hand the claim to truth which the church could not renounce and on the other the typically modern phenomenon of the plurality of religious and cultural experiences, all legitimated by the modern principle of freedom. The long and tortuous redactional process of the scheme indicates an important path towards the maturing of conciliar reflection on this theme: from the very first project entirely centred on the concept of 'tolerance' to the difficult elaboration by Monsignor De Smedt on the rights of the 'erroneous conscience', to the claim by Fr Courtney-Murray that the state had no competence in matters of religion. Finally, after the last discussion, the choice was made of a treatment which was not theological, but rather sought to respond to the demands which came from the world, in a perspective similar to that of scheme XIII. In the declaration, the principle of religious freedom remained founded on the dignity of the human person, and the arguments put forward were fundamentally in the natural order.[6]

The attitude towards the modern world which matured at Vatican II corresponded to the church's abandonment of a claim to truth based on a mass of undiscussed doctrinal traditions and on the authority of its own institution. On the one hand this indicated a choice of forms of presence in modern society extraneous to the principle of the *potestas indirecta* of the post-Tridentine tradition and related, rather, to solidarity with those in modern society who suffered the gravest consequences and injustices: on the other hand it denoted an acceptance of the method of reciprocal encounter as an instrument for affirming the validity of its own message of salvation. In the second place, the new attitude was translated into an acceptance and theological reinterpretation of what were recognized as basic and universal principles of the modern awareness. However, this positive endorsement of the values and principles of modern society ended up by leaving in the shade any facing up to its concrete and real problems, which were both characteristic and crucial. It is significant that despite the strong initial motivation, the conciliar documents then devoted relatively little space to the problem of the relationships between the developed and the developing countries; thus even the problem of demographic growth remained substantially unresolved, because it was authoritatively subsumed by the fathers under the discussion on birth control; in connection with religious freedom, the scheme of Monsignor De Smedt on the 'erroneous conscience', which considered the problem of religious and cultural plurality, albeit from a particular point of view, was rapidly set aside. Only modern war was fully discussed, but the very difficulties that arose over this question seemed to belie that the ideals of the modern conscience led to any effect judgment.

The difficult modernities of Paul VI

The Council ended with a series of messages addressed to different social categories, messages which in style and intention recalled the initial messages of October 1962. There was a concern that the 'dialogue' with the modern world set in motion by the Council should continue and deepen in subsequent years, and that a new stage of pastoral concern in the church should be inaugurated. However, the difficulties surrounding such dialogue soon became evident. The problem of the development of countries which had barely emerged from the process of decolonization became increasingly evident, while the Western countries had to cope with the problems of the new consumer societies and the progressive crisis of cultural values which exploded in the challenge from the young at the end of the 1960s.

In the years of the pontificate of Paul VI, the church was faced with the task of defining its role and position in modern society in new terms, but equally had to face the consequences of a process of secularization and modernization which deeply affected its very structures. With profound concern Paul VI drew attention to the risk of a progressive institutional and doctrinal fragmentation as a result of the particularistic character of the liturgical and institutional reforms wanted by the Council in certain regions, and to the contrasting developments of theological reflection and pastoral action. The most radical tensions arose from the differing interpretations of the conciliar documents. If on the one hand a minority of bishops found in Mgr Lefebvre the reference point for a minimalist reading of them, expressing a conservative attitude quite closed to modernity, on the other hand various experiences like that of the base communities which emerged in Latin America after the Medellín Conference traced in a re-reading of the Pastoral Constitution *Gaudium et Spes* and Paul VI's encyclical *Populorum Progressio* the motivations for deep involvement in the liberation movements in their countries. Faced with these developments, the *magisterium* of Paul VI was very cautious. Dialogue and encounter were certainly to remain the criteria for the attitude of the church. He himself devoted a very important part of his programmatic encyclical of 1963 to the theme of dialogue. However, it was Paul VI who emphasized with increasing stress in the years after the Council that dialogue did not mean losing the appropriate distinction between the church and the world. He pointed out many times that the church would in any case have to remain itself, that the baptismal promises called for some renunciation of the spirit of the world, and that the attitude of *aggiornamento* did not mean the abandonment of tradition, dogmas and ecclesiastical structures. He also often referred to the Pastoral Constitution, but always gave it a very prudent reading, wanting above all to avoid the risk of a sell-out of the traditional doctrine of Christianity. The difficulties of finding a prudent balance between the opposed choices finally led Paul VI to a progressive shift towards a more spiritual dimension of the mission of the church. The religious choice put forward in the opening allocution of the difficult 1974 Synod and then in the subsequent apostolic exhortation *Evangelii nuntiandi* seemed to indicate an appropriate criterion of separation between the church and the world, describing what was to be the presence of Christians in the world. This affirmed that the deepest identity of the church derived from its vocation to evangelization, and evangelization would have lost its *raison d'être* if it were removed from the religious axis which governed it. As he said: 'The kingdom of God before all else – in its fully theological sense.'[7]

Paul VI regarded modernity essentially as a crisis of traditional structures and values. However, his attitude was not just one of condemnation, but, following the indication already given at the Council, was also one of welcome to what were recognized as universal values in modern culture: a stress on justice for the people of the Third World, and on the principles of equality and freedom. However, he was more closed and rigid to certain concrete problems and particular situations. In the encyclical *Humanae vitae*, which faced the great problem of birth control that had been held in suspense during the years of the Council, the distinction desired between church doctrine and the values of the modern world was more evident. However, his attitude was different on questions of international politics. The affirmation of the model of a church free from all political bonds and interests paradoxically coincided with the Holy See achieving the utmost international prestige. Paul VI himself experienced this when he addressed the United Nations in October 1964. The problems of the Third World were the determining factor for the new form of the presence of the church in international relations. In this context the papal teaching began to take on the specific role of a moral authority and a custodian of the values of justice and human rights. By making himself the champion of such values, Paul VI could renounce the traditional aim of a specifically Christian international order, and could argue for the autonomy of religion from certain political choices. However, under his pontificate the Holy See gave a new boost to political concordats, making thirty of them.[8]

The new role of the church in the modern world according to John Paul II

The uncertainty and caution of Paul VI at any rate left room, in the *magisterium* of John Paul II, for a search for a stronger role for the church in culture and the modern world. By the middle of the 1960s the optimistic idea of economic progress which could lead to universal prosperity had unexpectedly collapsed: the oil crisis had noisily given the lie to the idea of a development which it had been thought could be limitless; in the summer of 1975 the Helsinki Conference had crowned the period of international *détente* in previous years, but barely two years later the difficult questions of missiles in Europe arose, and in 1979 the semi-failure of SALT 2 and the invasion of Afghanistan marked a serious halt to the *détente*. However, the renewed tension between the two blocks did not interrupt the slow process of the opening up of the Holy See towards Eastern Europe which had begun in the middle of the 1960s. It is within this basic perspective that the pontificate of John Paul II has to be analysed.

His social encyclicals have brought out quite a coherent magisterial project which has its cornerstone in a proposal for a Christian humanism capable of forming a substantial foundation for the multiplicity of modern cultural expressions. This humanism is not based simply on gospel principles, but on the presupposition that such principles are the common patrimony of human nature and history. They are said to have found their most significant historical expression in European civilization, laid down in the culture of Western and Eastern Europe, which represent the oldest form of the civilizations which have still remained faithful to their Christian foundation. In the words of John Paul II one can clearly recognize the ideal of a 'Christendom' which is to regain for the Catholic church its traditional role as the guarantor of fundamental principles, civil as well as religious. In the crisis of the great ideologies which have characterized modernity so far, the church seems to be indicating a quest for a new position which guarantees new areas and forms of Christian presence in society and a new Christian inspiration for social values, in a change from a religious legitimation of political institutions.[9]

This substantially anti-modern plan can be seen through a style imposed by John Paul II on his pontificate which does not lack features of undoubted modernity, like his frequent apostolic visits, his effective use of the mass media, the abandonment of any sacral aura around his person and the constant quest for direct contact with the masses and for occasions for the widest dissemination of his words. In general John Paul II has avoided emphasizing the primatial character of his *magisterium*, but despite his words he has assumed a quite special central position in the life of the church, and considerable prestige even in non-Christian circles, where he now appears in the garb of a modern religious leader. The importance of such forms of modernity is not to be underestimated, but in reality they do not disguise the most profound reasons for an attitude which goes in precisely the opposite direction.

It is significant that in putting forward the idea of Europe outlined above, John Paul II placed the emphasis more on its cultural and spiritual origins than on their modern developments, among which he has repeatedly castigated the negative aspects of secularization, the loss of a moral sense and the risks of technology. Stressing a direction already indicated at the Council and then by Paul VI, he has put a marked emphasis on the recognition of human rights, claiming them as a fundamental heritage of Christian teaching, but it is significant that he has avoided any direct reference to the Universal Declaration of 1789, limiting himself to speaking of that of 1948, which has been the civil foundation of post-war reconstruction.[10]

In the face of the most urgent challenges of modernity today, those represented by the emergence of a multi-cultural and multi-religious society and the new biological, energy and military technologies, the *magisterium* of John Paul II has shown itself ready for encounter, but always on the presupposition that the church is the respository of doctrinal and moral principles which are of universal value for all of human nature. The inter-religious encounter at Assisi, centred on the common prayer for peace, was quite significant from this perspective. It seemed to want to affirm the presupposition of the basic religious character of human beings and its effectiveness against the threats of modern war.

If we cannot speak directly of a condemnation of modernity, we need to recognize that in the *magisterium* of John Paul II modernity is judged in accordance with quite a rigid, distinctive scheme, applied either to its outcomes or its origins, which values in modernity only what can suitably function for affirming the new Christianity. The dialogue with the modern world which had been one of the most significant preoccupations of the Council still remains an effective objective in the life of the church, but it has proved more complex than could have been thought in the years of the Council, not so much as a result of the hostility shown by the world as by the depth to which the church has found itself unexpectedly involved in modernity and its crises and the difficulty of recognizing within itself a principle of identity which can justify its presence in history.

Translated by Mortimer Bear

Notes

1. Encyclical *Humanae salutis*, G. Caprile SJ, *Il Concilio Vaticano II* (2. vols.), Rome 1966, 258 (AAS 54, 1962, 5–13). See also the first announcement of the Council on 25 January 1959, AAS 51, 1959, 65–9, and the allocutions of 16 May 1962: *Discorsi, messaggi, colloqui del santo padre Giovanni XXIII*, Rome 1963, IV, 258, 806. For the whole question cf. G. Alberigo, 'Giovanni XXIII e il Vaticano II', in *Papa Giovanni*, Bari 1987, 211–43.

2. Caprile, *Concilio Vaticano II* (n. 1), AAS 54, 1962, 786–9. Critical edition: G. Alberigo and A. Melloni, 'L'allocuzione *Gaudet Mater Ecclesia* di Giovanni XXIII (11 Ottobre 1962)', in *Fede, tradizione, profezia. Studi su Giovanni XXIII e sul Vaticano II*, Brescia 1984, 185–283.

3. 'Schema Constitutionis dogmaticae de Ecclesia', in *Schemata Constitutionum et Decretorum de quibus disceptabitur in Concilii sessionibus – Series secunda*, Rome 1962, 7–90; 'Schema Constitutionis dogmaticae de deposito Fidei pure custodiendo', in *Schemata Constitutionum et Decretorum de quibus disceptabitur in Concilii sessionibus – Series prima*, Rome 1962, 25–69.

4. Paul Gauthier, *La chiesa dei poveri e il concilio*, Florence 1966.

5. Cf. Roberto Tucci SJ, 'Introduzione storico dottrinale', in *La Constituzione pastorale sulla Chiesa nel mondo contemporaneo*, Asti 1967, 15–134.

6. Cf. Jerome Hamer OP, 'Progressiva elaborazione del testo della Dichiarazione', in *La libertà religiosa nel Vaticano II*, Asti 1967, 15–134.

7. *Encicliche e discorsi di Paolo VI*, Rome 1976, XXVI, 642; AAS 66, 1974, 562. The apostolic exhortation is in AAS 68, 1976, 5–76.

8. For the pontificate of Paul VI cf. *Paul VI et la modernité dans l'Eglise. Actes du colloque organisé par l'École française de Rome (Rome, 2–4 juin 1983)*, Rome 1984.

9. D. Menozzi, 'Vers une nouvelle Contre-Réforme?', in *Le retour des certitudes. Évenements et orthodoxie depuis Vatican II*, Paris 1987, 292.

10. P. Ladrier, 'La vision européenne du pape Jean-Paul II', in *Le rêve de Compostelle. Vers la restauration d'une Europe chrétienne*, Paris 1989, 174.

The Strategies of Reconquest in the New Europe and the Impossibility of Getting Past Secularization

Jean-Louis Schlegel

It is natural, after all, for the supreme head of a great religion or a great church to be concerned to increase – or at least not to check – the number of those who hear his message or to remove obstacles in the way of the life and growth of the community for which he is responsible. That, as they say, is his role. So one should not criticize the pope for being preoccupied with the spiritual, religious, Christian, indeed strictly Catholic future of Europeans. Nevertheless, the question of objectives and means remains – unless he is credited with infallibility in these matters too (and there is no lack of people who do indeed think him infallible here, nor are they necessarily marginal in the Catholic church).

In fact, the pope's own project raises a number of questions. Does John Paul II really want to 'reconquer' Europe, a Europe which is thought to have deserted its Christian 'vocation'? Does he want to remake a 'Christian Europe' which would be a kind of 'Christendom' of the modern era? If that is not the case, what is the pope doing, what does he want when he speaks of a 'new evangelization' of Europe, and when a recent synod goes into this idea in some detail? And if this 'dream of Compostella',[1] as it has been called, really exists in the pope's head, has it any chance of success? What will be the means for achieving it?

Within the framework of a brief article it is impossible to expound in its complexity the thought of John Paul II on this issue and the questions that it raises – though one could describe it quite clearly. So I shall attempt mainly to indicate a set of problems in the direction indicated by the title of this article, taking up official declarations on the 'new evangelization' (so as not to focus the question solely on the pope) and then offer a more global evaluation of the problem posed by John Paul II's 'new evangelization'.

The new 'evangelization' as a 'metapolitical function' of Christianity

In a recent interview,[2] shortly before the 'Special Assembly for Europe of the Synod of Bishops', Cardinal Lustiger, Archbishop of Paris, dismissed as 'fantasy' the charge that the pope wanted to reconquer Europe. The 'dream of Compostella' did not reveal either the intention of the pope or the situation of the churches. For these churches, the new evangelization would be above all a 'right to speak' in European debates, in particular in the moral debate which 'is now taking place at the heart of European societies'. The role of the churches would be to 'bring into play the fundamental factors of social life, i.e. the non-political (or metapolitical) forces of political life'. For example, the churches would have an essential role to play in the restoration of memory to the East in those nations whose history had been manipulated. Or again, in connection with the European past of wars and violence, the churches would have to accept mutual forgiveness for sins committed. They would also have a caritative function in Eastern and Western Europe, through their associations, in correcting the 'new poverties', in other words the negative effects of an 'economic logic which is cruel to the weakest'. Mgr Lustiger ended by asking (whom?) for Christians to be able to 'intervene for their own good and the common good. It is important to let Christians speak, not only because it is their right but also because it is in the interest of all.'

One would readily subscribe to these propositions, except that for the most part they are based on a fiction. What is preventing Christians today, not only in the West but even in the East, from fulfilling the 'metapolitical' (or metareligious) function in society of which Cardinal Lustiger speaks? He puts the blame on anonymous societies or states, claiming that they are opposed to the intervention of the churches in civil life. But the problem lies elsewhere, and moreover here we touch on one of the motives behind the church's treatment of secularization: civil societies and democratic states as such are arraigned and accused even when their responsibility for certain social and political failings has not been demonstrated and when they show neither the desire nor the impulse to maltreat or do away with the churches. The church has invented a kind of enemy for itself.

In my view the modes of social and political intervention which Cardinal Lustiger calls for do not pose any specific problem for the West, and less and less so for the East if the democratic process goes on. Even in a very 'lay' country like France, significant developments have taken place in this direction during the last century. The problem lies elsewhere: it is that of the vitality of the churches and the legitimacy that they are capable of giving themselves in the public democratic sphere to back up their actions and their words. What is at stake is not so much the content as the form of a presence, and that also goes for the ethical debate: the church is not forbidden to speak, but it is asked about the forms of its interventions and the way in which it develops its doctrine and its decisions in these spheres.

The 'new evangelization' as the institution of a more Christian civilization

In its final message,[3] the recent synod of bishops for Europe returned to the 'new evangelization'. Although the idea of a 'programme aimed at a "restoration" of the Europe of yesterday' was explicitly rejected, one can find some strange formulae in this document. Thus we are told that, faced with the practical atheism and materialism implicitly dominant in Europe; faced with the explosion of new forms of religion showing a 'desire for religious experiences', 'the whole of Europe faces the decision to make a new choice for God'. But who is the subject 'Europe' which is thus summoned to make a choice for God?[4] In the same direction, after stressing the Christian roots of Europe, roots which have fashioned it to a greater degree than any other influence, the text rejects the idea of taking up as it was a Christian heritage from a bygone past. However, it adds that Europe must 'find the capacity to decide anew on its future in the encounter with the person and message of Christ'. If it has to avoid all 'restoration', it must nevertheless, the document says, 'institute a more profound civilization, i.e. one that is more Christian and, consequently, also more richly human'. But again, to what 'Europe', to whom in Europe, is this appeal being made?

The difficulty lies in the 'more'. If the document means that Europe, through its states and nations and even more its individuals, must continue to be inspired by fundamental values, by the 'fundamental principles of humanity' which arose from a Christian matrix, who would not subscribe to such a perspective? Among these principles, the text itself lists 'above all the concept of the transcendent God . . . the new and very important notion of the dignity of the human person; fundamental human brotherhood . . . ' But it is quick to add that under the pressure of rationalism these values and these principles have been preserved in such a way that they rest on a purely immanent foundation (reason): hence they have become fragile (a fragility proved concretely, according to the document, by the events of the twentieth century), and the objects of controversies and debates.

In this context it is not enough for Christians to propagate these 'Christian values' like justice and peace; they must proclaim Christ himself, and thus the church must be implanted or reimplanted in Europe.

All the more since in the European context 'the process of secularization is so far advanced that evangelization must be taken up again almost "as zero"'. Besides, evangelization thus understood 'must affect not only individuals but cultures', so that 'the evangelization of a culture implies the "inculturation" of the gospel'. Reference is made for this inculturation to the challenge represented by 'the new cultural facts of Europe, marked by modernity but also by what is called "post-modernity"'.

The word 'reconquest' is absent from this text, so one cannot criticize it on this point, though we should ask once again at whom these words are aimed: it always seems to be Europe, a kind of abstract entity, a civilization and culture from which the real people of Europe, Europeans as they are, have disappeared. In any case, like so many other documents which talk of evangelization, this is a text totally given to self-reference, in which the reality to be evangelized disappears in general ideas and cavalier perceptions (like the failure of Enlightenment reason, which is stressed once again); or affirmations which have become intrinsically problematical are dealt out without any concern to demonstrate them. Thus it is stated that 'anyone who does not know the true and living God does not know man', or that a Christian civilization is 'more richly human'. In context, this phrase can be understood. Nevertheless, even if one takes account of the homiletic literary genre of the document, it does not fit in well, and appears purely as a counter to those innumerable people in European culture who say the opposite. One would have liked more humility, i.e. more concern to legitimate the statements advanced. But how can those be humble who shrug off, as this document does once again, all true responsibility for the misfortunes which have come upon Europe since the advent of the 'fragile foundation' of enlightened reason, and see themselves outside the 'catastrophic' heritage of the Enlightenment?

A symptom: the exclusion of 'critical theologians'

Generalities? Indeed, but generalization has its limits: there are details in the text which say a good deal about the real conception of the new evangelization. Thus it is specifically said that all in the church (bishops, priests, lay, religious, parishes, small communities, new religious movements . . .) are involved in responding to the challenge of modernity and post-modernity. All . . . except 'certain worrying theological tendencies', since 'theological discord is an obstacle to the undertaking of this evangelization, in particular the evangelization which has constantly to be pursued within the church itself'. Only 'theology rooted in the Word of God and adhering to the *magisterium* is very useful for the mission of evangelization'. Elsewhere it is again said that to respond to the challenge of modernity and postmodernity, contributions will be needed from 'men from the world of culture' and 'theologians who are at heart in communion with the church'.

Let us pass over the pettiness of the remarks and the almost slanderous allusions (the theology challenged is not rooted in the Word of God). The exclusion of the theologians indicates very precisely where, in the church, the intellectual debate on the 'new evangelization' is situated: in meetings of 'teams' or in spectacular encounters with intellectuals who are not believers or who are remote from the church. For the new evangelization, the gaze certainly needs to be turned outwards. But it is important at the highest point to keep to this externality so as not to be affected within, to disguise all internal plurality. So it is essentially a matter of taking the Christian message outside, into external culture. The 'inculturation' evoked, which might suggest a reciprocity of modern culture in the direction of the church, would then seem to be a rhetorical proposal. In this way the church is depriving itself without feeling of the intellectual and spiritual substance of theologians who in their intellectual activity have an intense *experience* of modernity and post-modernity, who hear in the strict sense the question of atheism and unbelief, for the benefit of those whose chief merit is to think like John Paul II. According to this document, the difficulties which have arisen in the ecclesial community – viz. theological dissonances – are due to the 'widespread phenomenon of a certain subjective reduction', to the alignment of the word of God and the church 'on the needs of such and such'. Anyone who wants to drown his dog says that it has rabies!

What about secularization?

As I said earlier, I shall not be analysing the theme of the 'new evangelization' in the statements of John Paul II here. That has been done elsewhere.[5] In my view, the interview with Cardinal Lustiger quoted above and the synodical document are indubitably drawing back from some much more precise affirmations made by the pope over the past years. Above all the Archbishop of Paris, but also the synod on Europe, are in fact taking account of the lively criticisms made both in the Catholic church itself and in the other Christian churches, as well as in non-Christian spheres. Nevertheless, basic questions remain which are not removed by the corrections and nuances introduced, and which leave one sceptical about the project of the new evangelization and its chances of success.

In particular, there is a marked ambivalence, not to say ominous confusion, over the notion of secularization. As currently understood, secularization indicates that whole sectors of reality – politics, society, culture, the economy, law, teaching – have progressively detached themselves from the religious sphere and thus become autonomous – in their functions and their decisions. They no longer depend on religious criteria and in principle respond to criteria established through reason, in particular by the rationality of 'means and ends'. It may be that secularization will never be finished, that consequently total autonomy is a utopia or an impossible dream of modernity, that the government of individuals and institutions by reason alone is a mirage. But fundamentally this process really brought modernity into being and is a symbolic designation of it. In itself it is not in any way anti-religious: even if it has come about concretely through sometimes very violent historical conflicts and convulsions, the 'social end' of Christianity does not signify the end of Christian faith in consciences, either theoretically or in practice. It is easy to understand how the weakening of social and cultural support has consequences for the faith of individuals, not to mention that some aspects of modernity exercise strong pressure on the social and individual form of Christianity (in the sense of privatization, for example): nevertheless, in a world which has become secular the faith of many people can still remain alive and active. In one perspective one can even say that faith finds itself 'liberated' from its sacral yoke or from 'social religion', finally to accept itself with the risks and opportunities of freedom and a truth which, while indeed received from tradition, is also discovered in new dimensions. In this sense the religions, and notably Christianity, can recognize the 'legitimacy' of secularization as responsible autonomy, even from their point of view. Moreover, in spite of the long resistance of Catholicism the question has long been raised of the involvement of Christianity as such in the advent of secularization.

Of course the discussion remains open in the sociology of religion, not to say in political philosophy, about the nature, forms, extent and consequences of secularization. In the 1980s, it was even sharpened by the fact of the 'return of the religious', which put in question schemes which were too simply linear or over-hasty confirmations of the scheme from the previous decades (for example, confirmation by the diminution of practice, the crisis of 'vocations', the weakening of religious authority, etc.). We do better to note that modernity was more complex than people believed, that there were modernities in the plural (scientific, technological, political and cultural) which did not coincide in either time of space, and also that rationalization was not univocal in all spheres or even in the same sphere. On the other hand the (alleged) failure of 'modernity', the (supposed) entry into a 'post-modernity' with other types of relationship to the religious, the sacred, etc., have become important themes in the debate on the place of religions in contemporary society.

The 'great story' of Christian Europe, of its disappearance and its return

In short, one gets the impression that in the theme of the 'new evangelization' of Europe all these distinctions disappear. All analysis, all appropriation and all criticism of historical, sociological and philosophical knowledge of modernity, of secularization and of rationalization, is dispensed with, to appear at a very different level: that of a 'great story' about Christian Europe and about the religious value judgment which derives from it. In this perspective the theme of secularization is primarily thought to be negative.

The 'great story' is that of the Christian roots and the 'ideal unity of the European continent under the aegis of Christianity'. There is no point here in asking about the truth of 'Christianization' and the nature of mediaeval Christianity. This is a myth of origins, with its undifferentiated universe. There is a desire to retain of the 'happy encounter' between Europe and Christianity only the positive values bequeathed by Christianity to modern Europe, to European humanism (values which are still listed by the recent synod, see above), while retaining only the negative sides of secularization. These Christian values are certainly themselves secularized; from now on they are based on a purely immanent foundation; but at root there is no rupture. The best in Europe remains Christian, but Europe no longer knows it. Hence the catastrophes which have already struck and the risk of even greater ones in the future.

In the language of the pope, in particular, secularization – often denoted by the term 'secularism', with its ideological, active and pejorative connotations – is largely confused with the rise of militant or implicit atheism and with de-Christianization,[6] understood above all as an active rejection of the Christian faith. So secularization, as mixed up with atheism, materialism and the indifference of the masses, seems to relate to a *choice* by Europe. But this 'death of God' has ended up also in more recent times in signifying the 'death of man'. Thus there is a stress on the ominous anthropological consequences of secularization: the loss of direction (moral), of freedom, of truth, of 'communion' (brotherhood and solidarity) – in other words, on the spiritual crisis of the European West which in turn justifies the 'new evangelization'. The reconciliation between Europe and Christianity seems to be the remedy to these evils, brought about, according to an increasingly accepted explanation, by the Enlightenment as a source and drama of 'atheistic humanism'.

I have already emphasized that the current spiritual crisis is globalized. It too is part of the 'great story', and can be subjected to a variety of analyses. This lack of differentiation makes it possible, for example, to talk of a crisis of civilization identical 'on both sides to the old dividing line between opulence and indigence, between liberalism and totalitarianism' (Cardinal Lustiger, in the interview quoted above). We know that this identification made by numerous delegates to the recent synod nevertheless ended up by prompting criticisms and resistance.

As in the case of the beginning (the Christian roots of Europe) and the middle (the process of secularization), the (present) end of this story is taken up into a pessimistic, not to say apocalyptic, view of the future of European societies. Thus 'Europe' is as it were called on and addressed as a global agent or a unique entity, as a person with self-awareness, to remember its Christian roots and to restore Christianity (Catholicism?) as a specific source of its ethical inspiration. In fact the discourse is ambivalent: these people say they do not want a 'restoration'; they claim to respect the autonomy of the state; they reject (as at the time of the visits of the pope to Strasbourg and Sweden) an integralist church which would want to tell the state what to do. However, everything continues as if there were implicitly a call to the European state, democratic and lay, to restore Christianity as a transcendent foundation. These people act as if the democratic state had in some way *decided* positively to evacuate Christianity, and thus as if it were *actively* practising atheism and religious indifference (this point of view is wrong even in France, which is very lay). From all sides, through all the lines of the texts and through the practical decisions one feels this massive fact: autonomy is not a value for the pope and those advocating the new evangelization.

The new religious movements since the 1960s, first in the USA and then in Europe, have been interpreted as an implicit response to the multiple crisis in the West during these years and still today. Here, in the framework of the new evangelization, the church is explicitly putting itself forward as the *solution* to a crisis which is often dressed, as I have said, in apocalyptic colours (people preach in the name of the preservation of the future). Instead of seeking with others to understand the involutions, the weaknesses, perhaps the decay of democracies and liberal societies; instead of being fully involved as also an heir of the democratic, liberal, advanced, etc. Europe, in order to propose remedies to the difficulties, the church of the new evangelization is proposing its version of a philosophy of history to which it is the ultimate key.

It is not the 'great story' as such which is the issue: one can understand how a mobilization implies a discourse of a homiletic or paraenetic kind, with a rhetoric of its own. However, for all that, it cannot say just anything. We can best see the perverse effects of talk of the 'new evangelization' from its results in the church itself. I shall leave aside the more than questionable nominations of bishops or the exclusion of nonconformist theologians from teaching posts: this practice gives some idea of the understanding that people in high places have of the 'new' evangelization. But when one sees the reactions from 'ordinary Christians' one gets two impressions: either this talk of 'Christian Europe' rings no bells, quite simply because no one can see the concrete form that these incantatory appeals can possibly take, or it mobilizes exclusively groups (young people in particular) with a traditionalist tendency, with sectarian (in the sociological sense of the word) traits, narrowly identified with the words of John Paul II, and in effect with a conception of the Catholic conquest or reconquest of the secularized societies of Europe. Nor will I mention here the vast uneasiness which has been created in the other Christian confessions and in non-Christian religions (Judaism, for example) or among unbelievers. The minimalist, 'metapolitical' discourse of the Archbishop of Paris belies all this. But also, there could be no better indication, in my view, of the likely failure of the 'new evangelization'. Moreover, we can see the impossibility from now on not only for Christianity but also for the other great religions of humanity (Islam, Buddhism, etc.) to want to identify or reidentify themselves with the continents and countries which saw their historical expansion.

Translated by John Bowden

Notes

1. Cf. the symposium *Le rêve de Compostelle*, Paris 1989.
2. *Le Monde*, 13 November 1991, 2.
3. Cf. *Documentation Catholique* 2043, February 1992, 123–32.
4. *Le Choix de Dieu* is the title of a book by the Archbishop of Paris, Mgr Lustiger, which has enjoyed considerable success in France (Paris 1987). The influence of the Archbishop can be recognized in the redaction of the final document of the synod. As to the concrete *meaning* that the fomula might have here, it is to be understood that the European states must recognize a transcendent foundation to their constitutions and their laws, or recognize 'that a system of fundamental values based on Christianity is their precondition', as Cardinal Ratzinger says (cf. *Eglise, oecuménisme et politique*, Paris 1987, 288). But what is the difference between this and the 'Christian state' of a short while ago?
5. Cf. in *Le rêve de Compostelle* (n. 1) the article by René Luneau and above all the one by Paul Ladrière; cf. also my study 'L'Europe chrétienne de Jean-Paul II', *Esprit*, November 1990, 109–25. Each article has a large number of quotations.

6. De-Christianization is not analysed any more than secularization (and the initial Christianization). It is above all a voluntary, ideological or practical detachment from the doctrine and the norms of the church. At most it is recognized that atheism itself is a phenomenon inherent in Christianity (cf. the references in my 'L'Europe chrétienne', n. 5). But in connection with the estrangement of the church, no attention is paid to the analyses of historians who agree on the essential role of Jansenism, of church rigorism in general in connection with the limitation of births. Cf. Roger Chartier, *Les origines culturelles de la révolution française*, Paris 1990, 116–37; for the recent period, Emmanuel Todd, *L'invention de l'Europe*, Paris 1990, 447–50. Chartier talks of 'religious discourse turned against themselves by faithful powerless to observe its demands'.

Opportunities for the Christian Message in Tomorrow's World

Paul Valadier

From the moment of its birth, Christianity was thought to be dying. In his second letter to the Corinthians (chapter 6), Paul reports this diagnosis – not without irony: they think that we are dying, yet we live! Such a pessimistic judgment has constantly been echoed over two thousand years, and there is no reason for it to disappear at the dawn of the third millennium. On the contrary, today the future of Christianity seems very threatened, uncertain and this time compromised, though doubtless less because of the weaknesses and betrayals of the church than because of its inability to put its message across effectively to contemporary minds.

Before assessing the opportunities for the Christian message, we should also note the very considerable force of the challenge. Even if all the uncertainties about the future cannot be reduced to such a diagnosis, it does seem that the most serious disquiet stems from the fact that modernity has in some way voided the Christian message of its power and its relevance. Modern culture is not essentially hostile to Christianity, thus robbing it of a situation of conflict which it could exploit by defining itself in relation to an opponent! Rather, modern culture is either indifferent to or, infinitely more serious, marked by Christian 'values' in relation to human beings, by a tendency towards non-violence, both of which structure the democratic debate and the procedures of rational argument or communication; it is also marked by a concern for the universal and for an improvement in the human condition, to the point of being able to do without a message the essential contribution of which it has already integrated. Basically inspired by Christianity itself, this modernity for the most part owes its direction to Christianity, but at the cost of the extinction or dilution of the matrix through which it was communicated. That was the diagnosis already made by Nietzsche in the previous century. Suddenly, Christians either have the painful impression of being dispossessed of their own message and no longer having anything to 'contribute' to society, or they take refuge in the apocalyptic visions of the present, 'the torture chamber in which we are now imprisoned',[1] which, by making them accusers, restores some meaning, albeit quite negative, to their presence.

The hypothesis I want to put forward here is quite the opposite of these discouraging prognoses. Leaving aside the debate on the debt of modernity to Christianity, and accepting that many features of our societies would be intelligible without a reference to their Christian source, I shall argue, rather, that so-called modernity can provoke Christianity to disclose a number of its potentials which are hidden or paralysed. If Christianity is able without fear and naivety to enter into a positive relationship to modern society, it will derive renewed energy in this process or this confrontation.

The specific religious character of Christianity

According to their most essential logic, religions are led to propose or to impose as complete a framework as possible for society through a system of rules, norms and laws, thought to derive from the divine will. This legalistic tendency makes religion the source of social norms and the basis of the bond between human beings, and their bond with nature and the deity. Now it is impossible not to note the point at which the message of Jesus opposes such an enveloping of the social by the religious, or more precisely the point at which it shifts legalistic perspectives by subordinating them to human well-being.[2] The emphasis on the heart as the place of true faithfulness to the will of God certainly does not minimize the importance of the law, but it does bring an upheaval in the hierarchy of values the scope of which we can certainly see better today. In this way Jesus in fact puts in question the mode of the presence of a religion in society, and if the domination of a religious model which wants the church to provide the framework and the norm of social life in all its dimensions has managed to obliterate the scope of this message, modernity has virtually forced us to discover that the legalistic model has become inoperative, even dangerous.

One of the most beneficial effects of secularization, however ambiguous this term may be, is to show the real 'autonomy of earthly realities', i.e. specifically the impossibility of bending them to a heteronomous model, even a religious one, and the correlative need to respect the rationality inherent in them. In that sense this modernity which is so traumatic for those who dream of society having a religious framework (or the church as a framework) gives every opportunity to a religion with no ambition to impose a divine model on history. This message from modernity is indeed painful to hear, since it stirs Christians out of the old nostalgia of the religious model which dominated for so long and which, for that very reason, is thought to be intrinsically bound up with the very presence of Christianity in history. But it can be, and is, liberating, if it can rediscover for believers the real revolutionary tendency in Christianity in the relationship which it sets up between religion and society (economic, political, cultural). In this sense modernity necessitates a radical re-reading and reinterpretation of the nature of the presence of Christian religion in the structure of a society. At the same time it offers some opportunities for a more exact and authentic faithfulness to the gospel perspectives on the way to seek and honour the will of God.

A religion of freedom

Hegel showed in a convincing way that Christianity is the religion of modernity because it is also the religion of freedom.[3] Without adopting Hegel's theses on freedom and Christianity as they stand, we can at any rate accept the fruitfulness of his analysis. For modernity puts personal and public freedom at the centre of its perspectives and the values which it wishes to honour politically and culturally. In other words, it organizes itself from and around the promotion of subjectivity, understood as the aptitude of subjects to determine themselves freely and in awareness of a cause. Such an affirmation is doubtless utopian and even naive in the eyes of the detractors of modernity, but it is also a decision which we can always see better at the points where it has not been definitively taken once for all: this does not rob it of any of its relevance, but on the contrary gives it its sense of a utopian horizon. A political system is not solidly established, any more than democracy is, unless responsible citizens constantly give it life, and freedom or subjectivity are positive values only if they are desired and honoured anew by men and women who opt for them rather than for passivity, caprice or servitude.

Now the Christian message can be perfectly at ease with these perspectives. Does it not put at its centre the idea of the free adherence of believers to the Word of God presented to them? Does not Christianity rightly claim to be a religion of freedom, and not primarily of the law?[4] Does it not call on its faithful to *become* children of God, to be willing to take the step of a liberation by which they undertake to assume little by little what they are? By closely associating the worship to be offered to God with love of neighbour, and by proclaiming with the evangelist John that the one who claims to love God without loving his brother is a liar,[5] the Christian message commends the service of others, and thus presents itself as an essentially ethical religion, i.e. one which makes a sense of responsibility towards others the criterion of faithfulness to God. Now here again modernity leads us to understand that such an ethical statute is particularly relevant in a society which presupposes and calls on responsible citizens. In this sense the commitment of believers, to use a somewhat hackneyed phrase, is the real sphere of worship that they offer to God by honouring their neighbour, more particularly by having a concern for the voiceless.

One might go on to add that modern freedom can decay into a caprice which kills freedom, that subjectivity can be confused with subjectivism, and that the sense of one's own value can be ruined by a radical individualism. In comparison with these dreadful distortions, Christianity is not too badly placed to offer a sense of human beings and society which avoid the evils into which our societies can easily sink. By the religious and moral education which it puts forward, it exalts freedom at the same time as telling people that they will lose themselves if they do not give themselves; it emphasizes the person at the same time as it asks people to enter into the life of a body where they will respond to their vocation by finding their true place in it; it cultivates a sense of responsibility by inculcating in the faithful that while they may legitimately seek their personal fulfilment, this cannot come about without promoting a collective life which each and everyone have their place. Through all these traits, the Christian message can find a place within modernity as a force for criticism and positive proposals, which can mobilize people for responsible freedom and thus be fruitful for social life. But how could Christianity manifest the vigour of its message and bring to modernity the counter-balance which it needs if it turned back on itself in mistrustful aggressiveness towards a modernity which nevertheless offers it its opportunities? This shows once again that modernity offers a favourable ground for the Christian message only if Christianity accepts present and future challenges, if it lets itself be provoked by them instead of imprisoning itself in verbal denunciations.

Logos and modernity

Democratic modernity presupposes that a truth is held to be such only if it has undergone the test of discussion and argument. On this point, in the last century John Stuart Mill anticipated what is held today by an audacious discovery about both the system of communicational reason (Habermas) and the procedures of falsification in the sciences (Popper).[6] He foresaw that modern reason would be that of an exchange regulated and founded on arguments put forward for discussion and the agreement of minds after the courageous verification of their opinions.

That is at least the principle, if not the reality, which in fact governs the democratic life of our societies.

Must we not see that in the internal demands on the exercise of this argumentative reason there is both a challenge and an opportunity for Christianity in that it is the religion of the Logos? There is certainly a challenge, in particular with relation to the dogmatic and moral discourse of the church: we can see how mistrust and fear of modern reason, wrongly identified with the critical reason of the Enlightenment, leads people to react by adopting an authoritarian style and tone, the most immediate effect of which in a democratic context is to devalue the Christian message. Now this challenge is only the other side of a beneficial demand which, if honoured, would lead straight to taking seriously the confession of the Logos, the creator of the natural and social bond, the persuasive power of which is recognized within relationships of interchange, in listening and in the rigour of conversation, in suggestions made freely and not imposed by threat or in the name of submission to a truth thought to come from on high. The Greek fathers loved to identify Christianity with reasonable religion, that which honours the Logos and which thus endorses the word as the constitutive place of all things which structures relations between God and human beings and also among human beings. They argued that the Christian message does not put forward any truth or practice which could not be recognized as sensible and just by a right reason, illuminated by the Spirit of the Word, and it is important for us to remember this lofty and demanding theological tradition and to be inspired by it.

Now there is no doubt that a modernity which endorses argumentative reason will lead to a theological reinterpretation of the Christian message, putting it entirely in the perspective of the Word offered, exchanged and shared, i.e. of a reactualization of this tradition. Here the Christian message will not make its mark on the margins of society nor in the nostalgia of a constraining or authoritarian model, but will take the same line as modern reason and contribute to making that reason fertile or to endorsing it, not from outside, but by free and critical acceptance of it as a model. By the same token, while the Christian message will always be presented as a religion, since one cannot dream of a non-religious Christianity, we must remember that the term 'religion' denotes a bond, and suggests at the same time that the social bond finds its source in a religious bond which is felt at the same time to be a human relationship, i.e. one in the immanence of history, as demanded by the logic of the incarnation.

'Our cohesion,' writes Jean-Marc Ferry, 'can no longer go through the sole *religere* of a "historical memory"; it must above all go through the *religere* of a "communicational ethics". It is there that the social bond appears in its pure matrix as the performance of a "communicational reason" for which any common basis of authority and inherited meaning can in principle be the object of doubt . . . That is also how communicational reason relates to the originating principal of religion.'[7] Is there not a challenge here which gives every opportunity to a religion of communication, presenting God himself as a personal relationship and placing God under the sign of the Word offered, proposed and possibly refused? Is this not the programme of a religion which shows its fertility and its sound basis, not by the imposition of a code of external laws but in the very dynamic of social relations?

Is there any need to add that this challenge for Christianity is a challenge for all religions? The very perspective of discussion or argumentative reason opens up a horizon of exchanges between religions which must do away with the risks of confrontation or sterile opposition. But here we have an issue in which Christianity can be eminently active: provided that it does not fear the life of the Logos, it could call on its conversation-partners to show an equal trust in the power of the word. Now this perspective not only opens up a renewed ecumenical horizon among Christians but without doubt forms the only authentic basis for a true relationship with the other great world religions. Which of them could meet the challenge of argumentation and the exchange of words without excessive risks?

The future of religion

The current system of reason to which I have just drawn attention also shows at what point the modernity of the twenty-first century will be different from the modernity of the preceding century. A rationalism which was intemperate, and to this degree not really faithful to the requisites of a sensitive reason aware of its 'limits', in the sense given to this term by Kant, would proclaim that religions will inescapably be obliterated from the horizon of modernity. There is no point here in recalling the many arguments put forward to postpone a disappearance which many people think inescapable and even desirable. It has to be noted that it is not so much the religions which are disappearing from the present scene, though they may be doomed to a certain death, as the ideological systems and the societies that they inspired. The philosophical criticism of totalitarianism indicates that a society risks becoming shut in on itself or considering itself (or its members) an object of limitless transformation if it obliterates its essential indeterminacy or if any power whatsoever seeks to occupy the void which nevertheless inspires it since the place is empty.[8] Here again there is a little-noted opportunity to rethink the presence of Christianity within a society, to the degree that it can be a factor of openness and otherness or represent an authority which can prevent a slide down the totalitarian slope by virtue of the otherness that it denotes.

From this perspective, if Christianity renounces the myth that it provides a social framework, the myth I mentioned earlier, and if in a positive way it undertakes to denote a freedom and otherness on which human beings cannot lay their hands but which as such assure within the heart of society the permanent presence of a reminder of the basis for all human research, it will be a force for constructive proposals and social intercourse. It will show that the religious attitude, far from being servitude or ignorance, is both sensible and relevant; that it is a way of setting oneself in the context of all things (God) and of the least of realities, that it inculcates a rejection of jealous and greedy appropriation and brings openness to the sense of otherness and of gift without which no human life is possible. In this perspective one could say that the Christian message inculcates a true sense of the sacred, which, accepted in faith, is not terror before the ineffable or the threatening, but respect for the highest value (in the eyes of God), human beings themselves and particularly the poorest, those whom a society which is too well policed and rationalized constantly risks forgetting or marginalizing as being *de trop*.[9]

The intellectual phenomenon of a modern society opening up the religious question in terms which would have disconcerted the rationalism of the last century gives every opportunity to a religion of gratuitousness or the sovereign grace of a God who calls us to his life by an invitation made to human freedom; however, it should be noted that along with this renewed openness goes a revival of ethical problems, so that by the same token such openness allows a quite favourable position to an essentially ethical religion. In fact the more a society moves in the direction of a differentiation of spheres, the further it pushes the development of the rationalities at work within it, the more problems of junctures or interactions inevitably arise within its very dynamic. It is impossible for genetic research not to raise serious anthropological, legal and moral problems; it is impossible for industrial development not to lead to reflection on our relationship to the environment. These questions are questions of relationship, of bond, of 'juncture', and, as I suggested earlier, as soon as one talks of relationships one enters the ground and the sphere of religion and ethics. Today's problems, and even more those of tomorrow, will be problems of relationship and meaning; dealing with them will oblige us to reopen a basic ethical reflection in which the Christian message can exercise its power of discernment and judgment. In this respect, too, far from marginalizing Christianity, the most advanced modernity will offer it possibilities of deriving new light from its ancient heritage.[10]

Conclusion

The liveliest faith does not free us from sounding out the future possibilities of the Christian message. It even requires us to ask ourselves how we can open up rational ways to a living presence, since God alone is free with his gifts and master of the future. It cannot be blind to very real obstacles. For while tomorrow's society offers particularly favourable ground for the Christian witness, there is no reason why Christianity, particularly in its Catholic version, should find ways of resurrection. To achieve that we shall have to do an immense amount of work in changing mentalities, engage in considerable intellectual effort to see that theology does not remain paralysed in the conceptualization of another age or paralysed by an anxiety to reproduce strictly the teaching of the hierarchy. More than anything else, there will be need for a sympathy, fully in keeping with the gospel, for today's men and women, as they are in their failings and in their greatnesses, touched by the tender regard of God. At a time when scorn for present society passes as the last word in ecclesiastical prophecy, one can be most deeply disturbed. But since the worst does not always happen, we can also hope that the Spirit of the living God will prevail over the defeatism of the prophets of misfortune, as it has done so often in the past.

Translated by John Bowden

Notes

1. Eugen Drewermann, *La parole qui guérit*, Paris 1991, 39.
2. In a number of passages, e.g. Mark 7.1–23 and parallels.
3. For example in the *Principles of the Philosophy of Right*, §124 or §185.
4. Forcefully systematized by St Paul in his letters to the Galatians and the Romans.
5. I John 2.
6. John Stuart Mill, *On Liberty*, London 1962, 141ff.
7. In *Christianisme et modernité*, Centre Thomas More, Paris 1990, ch. IX, 'L'ancien, le moderne et le contemporain', 267. Along the same lines, note the contribution by Joseph Moingt which forms ch. VI, 'Christologie et modernité', 169–87.
8. Claude Lefort has put special stress on these points, e.g. in *L'Invention démocratique. Les limites de la domination totalitaire*, Paris 1981, or *Essais sur le politique (XIX–XXe siècle)*, Paris 1986. One might also recall the analyses by Hannah Arendt.
9. In this connection cf. the profound remarks by Claude Geffré on the sacred in 'L'homme, une histoire sacrée', *Autrement* 127, February 1992, 'Dieux en société. Le religieux et le politique', 105–15.
10. Matthew 13.52.

'Post-Marxism' and 'Post-Modernity': What is the Church's Presence?

Paul Blanquart

A certain church is very relieved today. In Europe, and from Europe throughout the world, it had two great enemies: Communism in the East, with its militant atheism, and modernity in the West, with its dynamic of secularization. Now the first has just fallen in on itself and the second is very sick. We are, it is said, in a time of 'post-Marxism' and 'post-modernity'. In this new context, this church thinks that it can rediscover a social value which recent centuries denied it. An end of timidity, it proclaims, the way is largely open for a new evangelization. It remains to be seen what this evangelization is to consist of. For the gospel is good news, so the question is, what good does Christianity have to offer in connection with the present problems of our humanity? This question requires us to begin with a correct analysis of these problems.

First, what do we understand by 'post-Marxism' and 'post-modernity'? What has collapsed in the East is the totalitarianism of a party which claimed to combine in itself society, the state and knowledge. Even if other influences should not be neglected (notably the heritage of 'Asiatic' Russian despotism), it is beyond question that this political form has roots in Marxist thought. For Marxist thought, the Communist party is the organized working class (i.e. the great majority). And its doctrine is historical materialism, a theory of the future of society which attributes a privileged role to this class, that of liberating the whole of society by suppressing the exploitation of its work. How? By achieving collective ownership of the means of production (or socialism) through its dictatorship, a transition from the bourgeois state (that of capitalism) to the free association of workers (Communism, the stage at which, according to Lenin, the state should disappear). This party-class-knowledge-state was said to convey the meaning of history, and consequently was invested with a messianic power. Thus it derives from a nebula of 'great stories' of progress, very characteristic of the nineteenth century. Whereas the movement of modernity had consisted in an unlinking of what the symbolic and religious linked together into an integrated totality (cultural, political, economic, etc), these 'ideologies' made one of these autonomized elements (market, work, state, nation, reason) the determining vector for better tomorrows; they submitted, even reduced, the other to it. Here were new totalities, which one could describe as 'secular religions'. We know the evils and horrors which followed as a result.

The free market of economic liberalism, thought to enrich the whole world, led to the crushing of the weak by the strong. Scientific positivism made citizens passive, so that they put their lives in the hands of engineer technocrats and experts. And when the nation annexed to itself reason and the state, nationalisms ran riot, with Nazism at their head. At the starting point of Marx's thought there had been the idea of a relationship between the riches of some and the poverty of others, along with a moral rejection of this situation. That is not outmoded, and even now constitutes the prelude to any intellectual research which is concerned for justice. What is dead, justifying talk of 'post-Marxism', is the concentration in the working class of all the positive factors of history. With an inadequate idea of the state and its specific legal and political character, this approach made the working class a brute force, uncontrolled reason (Stalinism). And not respecting the autonomy of knowledge, it was unable to appreciate the modifications that this knowledge would introduce into the system of production, modifications which were to put in question the basic concepts of Marxism (the value of work, exploitation, proletariat), i.e. itself and its role.

Which brings us to 'post-modernity'. This term first of all appeared among architects and art critics who rejected the 'international style' and opposed it with a revival of all the forms of the past and from elsewhere (i.e. non-Western forms), mixing them up in the process. The result was praise for the diverse and the variegated, for heterogeneity and collage, against the linear progressiveness of functional reason which led to uniformity: the 'modern' on which they drew included on many of the 'great stories' mentioned above. The reason why the use of this expression has spread rapidly beyond these limited circles is that the attitude which it denotes corresponds to an experience which is now shared widely, thanks to the considerable development of means and techniques of communication, and to the general mixing of populations and cultures which follows. Different spaces and times are equally available, so people can play with them. However, these are all identities which by virtue of this fluidity have begun to float, frontiers which have become porous. Thus whereas formerly individuals had some consistency and solidity, now they are launched directly on currents which sweep them along, and no longer go by their roots but by their antennae. So how can the individual be anyone except by combining in a temporary and always open originality some of the possibilities offered? The 'I' (*je*) is also arrived at through a 'game' (*jeu*). No longer having any homogeneous universality, today it also cannot have anything of a closed totality.

So a serious risk occurs: that of not so much playing with the flux as being played with by it. We can see that clearly in the case of work. Just as our space presents itself more as a network of lines of communication punctuated by intersections, so industrial production conforms more and more to the model initiated by the petroleum industry: a network of tubes interspersed with globes in which liquids and gas are mixed and transform themselves. The inclusion of increasingly refined intelligence in equipment (electronics) allows an automation which increases productivity, at the price of excluding ancient craftsmanship. The result is a dual society: on the one hand there are those who dominate the flows upstream (research organizations, product and process planners) or downstream (marketing), and on the other those who are driven out. This is how technological progress is marginalizing the Third World. The metropolises of empires used to need the work of their inhabitants, which they exploited. Nowadays the developed zones do not require more than raw materials from the undeveloped zones, and then only until the time when they can replace these by synthetic materials which they develop themselves (and progress is already being made here). It is at this point that, quite independently of its totalitarian effects, the *tendency* of Marxism proves obsolete (though the old type of production still largely exists here and there). In these conditions, what use can the South still serve, except tourism? What does one do with those who are useless, unless they die, in order to nip their revolt in the bud? Some of the richer countries have found one answer for their nationals: to integrate those who have been excluded by means of social welfare payments and television (bread and games for second-class citizens). Where social welfare is not possible, in the Third World (where it would cost too much), there remains zombification (depersonalizing manipulation). There is flux everywhere, this time among cultures: by mixing them up, 'post-modernity' can make a brew perfectly adapted to being pumped all over the world by connecting pipes. The original works, which are taken up in this way, no longer have the substance given to them by particular creators, whether individuals or groups, but (if they are still identifiable, as they are in the best cases), are folklorized, reduced to images. Would it not be better to talk of 'neo-ancient' rather than 'post-modern'? It resembles, it is 'like'; it is no longer real, neither past, present nor from anywhere, but the appearance, the simulacrum, which is all the freer to circulate indefinitely, since it no longer relates to anything if it is nothing in itself. That, moreover, is the charge made against the architects whom I have mentioned: are not your arches, your columns and your façades simply stage props?

Are we in 'post-Marxism'? Certainly, but the social antagonisms are no less than those which Marx had rightly analysed. To put it simply, they are no longer of the same kind, since the reason for them has changed: the proletariat which had taken over the system of production (its strikes were effective) has been succeeded by the excluded who no longer have any means of action (apart from terrorism). Long live 'post-modernity'? That remains to be seen, since it bears within it the possibility of being absorbed by the image, hence the neutralization of the excluded through their zombification. As a result we can rejoice at the new situation only if we become capable of getting a society going which in our present intellectual and technological conditions has neither those who are excluded nor zombies. That amounts to saying that we must reinvent the social bond, avoiding totality on the one hand and the image and the brew on the other. Or again, we must hold together the linking (against exclusion) and unlinking (for creative autonomy). Modernity before the 'great stories' of the nineteenth century consisted in a long process of achieving autonomy, both for social life and for individuals. The French Revolution drew conclusions from this: detached from the religious and cosmic dimensions which embraced it, society could only fall in on itself, i.e. on individuals, themselves all free and equal. The principle was thus clearly presented, but at that time there was no way of translating it into a viable organization, hence the double and contradictory revolution which took place later, into political totalitarianism (on the pretext of equality, the social whole to the detriment of the individual) and economic liberalism (individual freedom to the detriment of social cohesion). Are we not better today at resolving this difficult problem?

I have said that the new individual has to make himself or herself (identity) out of the flux and through it (openness). To avoid being desertified, simply passed over or ignored by these same fluxes, from now anything local must link up with them, but in such a way as to make of itself something original which differentiates it in the global network. And the same is true of cultures: they can survive in their plurality only if they reinterpret themselves, each one under the impact of others, thus offering a number of particular features which are of general interest. In all spheres, then, it is important for conjunction and disjunction to go together. This is precisely what contemporary epistemology is trying to think about, under the twofold influence of biology and the information sciences, and the way in which they intersect.

Take the brain, which is a focal point of epistemological interest. This is a complex of flows of information, of connections and innovations, performing the more, the more it mobilizes all its neurones, i.e. each of them, to do its original work. These neurones are not linked together continually, but by synapses, a kind of gap, intermediary links which can be uncoupled. Thus it is not the same thing which circulates, but always something new, thanks to this 'between'. More broadly, that is the law of the living being: it organizes itself ceaselessly thanks to its openness to that which is not itself; it renews itself (autonomy) by being permeable to its environment (dependence) and distinguishes itself by changing. Here is a new status for the frontier which, like the skin, separates and holds together at the same time: life is a matter of exchange, of dialogue, not of closed totality or fusion.

Why not apply this approach to society, and envisage it as a 'social brain'? Moreover, do not people say that the intelligence is our new territory? Has not the grey matter become the principal productive force, and is it not by controlling it to their sole good that some people today are excluding others and making them zombies? So this society might be conceived of as a detotalized and open whole, as a living and continuous creation in which individuals and differentiated authorities (the market, the state, science) are connected in debate and interact equally by the exercise of a dialogical reason structured by the demand that they should all be active – economically, politically and culturally.

Not to go in this direction would allow what is becoming, day by day, one of the great contradictions of our era, to get even worse: at a time when, by virtue of the flux, we are committed to a logic of globality, ethnocentrisms are reviving everywhere. From now on the planet is one, imposing solidarity on all its inhabitants, who are responsible for one another and for the planet itself. This is an unprecedented pattern. The world was first made by a multiplicity of 'worlds', of cultures, without contact between them. Then it consisted of a vast field of forces in which states confronted one another, particularly in armed conflict, with a view to controlling territories bordering on frontiers which were heavily marked and guarded. Then it consisted in 'world economies', which ignored the ancient limits and in which, by the action of merchants and financiers, more or less distant centres and peripheries articulated themselves in an inegalitarian way. Today there is only one market in which the transnational bodies are entangled in competition, and the way in which they deal with the flux is to the detriment of the majority and threatens the life of the earth (desertification, an excess of arms to defend this exclusive system). Since globalization is now what it is, movements are developing against it everywhere which are calling for a step backwards, to the nation defined ethnically and culturally. Thus in the Third World tribal, racial and religious integralisms are reaffirming their own special identities against what in Iran they call 'Westoxication' (pollution by the West). In the decomposed Soviet sphere, where the imperial power had made a mosaic of people coexist by force, the old quarrels are surfacing again, often in a bloody way. In Western countries an extreme right-wing nationalism is being reborn which feeds on the fear engendered by global flux (immigration, unemployment) and calls for the closing of frontiers. So the dilemma is a simple one. Do we go on until things blow up, i.e. in the direction of generalized war (our world, in which everything today is interlinked, is a vast Bosnia-Herzegovina) at the risk of a destruction of the planet? Or can we construct a world society in which everyone can live (i.e. be themselves, even within the changes), and the world can live as well?

So that is the context, 'post-Marxist' and 'post-modernist'. For Christianity to bring good news within it requires it to contribute a dynamic which both loosens links and makes them, which escapes both the fate of particular totalizations and the illusory magma of the image. Is that the case with the 'new evangelization' as it is presented by the current pope? John Paul II is indubitably haunted by the dramas of our time (the increase in the gulf between rich and poor, the excess of arms) and by the threats that they pose to the future of humanity. But the central piece of reasoning by which he justifies his enterprise is the attribution of all recent evils (political totalitarianism, scientism and economic liberalism) to the modern concern to become free of God. Since modernity is thus identified with the tragic effects of the 'great stories' of the nineteenth century, to attack them (which should be done) amounts to opposing it, i.e. the very process of unlinking. Shaping society thus requires us to go backwards to the symbolic religious totality of before modern times. We know what importance this pope attaches to a reference to high mediaeval Europe: it was one through culture, Christianity being this culture. And we can understand that for a Pole, society = culture = religion: often deprived of a state, it was as a nation, by its culture, Catholicism, that his country was able to survive. But in that case we ought to be fully aware of the implications of this holistic conception, which ignores the autonomy both of individuals and of the various authorities of social life. On the one hand, if it is religion which guarantees a society its internal coherence, it is also religion by which this society is distinguished from others. As a result, apart from accepting a universal culture and religion from the start, which clearly does not correspond to reality, the relationships between societies, made inevitable by the flux, are doomed to lead to the absorption of some into the integrated totality of others. In that case we are back in wars of religion (e.g. Christianity against Islam and vice versa) in a way which is spurred on by the current revival of integralisms, and made worse by nationalistic claims in the name of the defence of cultural identities. On the other hand, these societies with a religious foundation were intrinsically inegalitarian: in them each person insisted on his rank, depending on sex, profession, etc. (in short, his status) in a hierarchical order (one need only think of Aristotelian natural law taken up by Christianity, or French society before the Revolution, etc.), inseparably divine, cosmic and social. This quite clearly does not correspond to the present demands of a world society which is both one and many, and in which all are active in the flux, and thus both equal and different.

But, it may be asked, is that the pope's position? Can one identify John Paul II with the nineteenth-century popes who, contrary to modern freedoms, favoured a restoration of the old order, culminating in the authority of the church? Far from being traditionalist, some people argue, he is suggesting an alternative 'post-modernity' to a modernity which has proved incapable of keeping its promises: so he is in front, not behind. It is true that the pope has a charismatic aura. And the adepts of this Catholic Pentecostalism are incontestably today's people: new individuals, they make use of the flux for their own personal lives. But how? By seeking, within cosy groups, an emotional experience which transports them. Preferring emotionalism to intelligence, they establish a bond among themselves of a fusional kind. That does not encourage a critical spirit and political concern. It has been noted that if in the poor countries these currents bring together above all the marginalized who are doomed to powerlessness, in the rich countries they are chiefly of interest to elements which are completely integrated economically. Might that not be because they aim much more to provide psychological help for each person where he or she is (regardless of whether they benefit or are excluded) in the present fluidity than to put in question the dualization which it brings in its train? Is not the unity thus achieved more imaginary than real? And do we not find ourselves back in the 'post-modern' brew? In the end of the day the church of John Paul II is a strange combination of the day before yesterday and today. Looking backwards, he still hopes that it will embrace a single humanity. But since restoration is impossible, he follows the taste of the day: so he has embarked on a logic of the image, more media-style than effective. He is neo-ancient.

A particular integrated totality, homogeneous universality, fusion: these three formulae have in common a refusal to take note of the unlinking brought about by modernity before the 'great stories'. The behaviour of the church down the centuries was such that people have ended up believing that this unlinking, and hence modernity, took place in the face of Christianity. But it in fact originates in Christianity. The Christian understanding deconstructed the ancient cosmic hierarchical totality: the creation is not an emanation nor a Neo-Platonic procession from the superior to the inferior, nor light which is degraded with each reflection: it is a break, a discontinuity between the creature and its creator. When human beings were defined by their degree on the scale of beings, this made them subjective powers, responsible for themselves. How then does one abstract from the modern disjunction of reality into three poles: God, absolute, i.e. unlinked, transcendence; nature, which God no longer inhabits and which becomes the object of science; and man, the individual subject both over against God and without God, who makes a contract with his kin to form society, and who undertakes to work nature by making use of the knowledge of its laws? But this unlinking is a new way of making a link. How? In the register of free grace. It is true of God himself. One, he is trine: these three persons are equal; they are not transitory distinctions within the deity but eternal differences. It is also true of human beings: they are all brothers and sisters, i.e. equal and different, both free and responsible. It is true, finally, of the unity between God and humanity: God is present to people, distinct and distinguishing them by keeping himself between them; he comes to them in the space of the word (of communication), in Christ, himself composed of two natures, divine and human, both inseparable and not confused. Thus the bond is also a remove: it is a 'between', between 'others'. Do not the Gospel texts speak to each person of a new birth by welcoming the other? In conversation, each opens himself or herself to the other without being absorbed by the other and as a result undergoes transformation, being differentiated both from the other and from his or her own former state. It is the same with the fate of a common humanity, diverse and inventive, made by and for all. So for the church to contribute to the solution of the problems of our time it is enough for it to be Christian. It is by re-establishing, in this reason which links by unlinking, its original alliance with modernity that it can help modernity to succeed.

What are the great challenges of the hour? To combat exclusion and zombification there is a need for democracy (everyone active). To combat the reductive 'great stories' there is a need to safeguard both autonomy and the competition of various authorities in social life: the market is not the state, and neither the market nor the state are science, but they need the others for society to live and make them exist. To combat religious fundamentalisms and ethnic nationalisms there is a need to promote reciprocal openness between cultures in such a way that each reinterprets itself for the good of a modernity which is both communal and burgeoning. To combat the destruction of the ecosphere there is a need to put nature and human beings in a position of partnership, embarked on the same adventure. In all these cases the frontier has to be transformed from being a barrier which encloses, a limit at which people confront one another for mutual destruction, into a communication by the grace of which each entity, individual or otherwise, renews itself for the benefit of all. It is the inter- which is interesting. The gospel is good news today since it sees life is played out in the respiration of frontiers, in their work of alternation. So the function of the church is to be a frontier crossing, at the service of all the interests of dialogical reason. And that means that it does not identify with anything which it puts into the dialogue. It cannot be a culture, a territory into which one enters and dwells. Its particular character is that of a leaven for a humanity-world in which all understand one another, each in their own language.

Translated by John Bowden

Special Column 1992/6

Correspondence in Communion

Papal encyclicals are, like all products of human history, subject to change in length and character, in frequency and purpose; they have changed often in the past, and it is now high time that they should change again.

In 1964, in an address announcing his forthcoming first encyclical, Pope Paul VI described an encyclical as 'a document in the form of a letter sent by the Pope to the bishops of the entire world: *encyclical* means circular. It is a very ancient form of ecclesiastical correspondence that characteristically denotes the communion of faith and charity that exists among the various "churches".'

As Paul VI went on to make quite clear, his description indicated an ideal type rather than an unchanging fact. Thus, although such letters were occasionally issued in the early centuries, encyclicals as we know them are a modern invention, beginning with Benedict XIV's letter of 3 December 1740 on 'the duties of bishops'. Moreover, more than half the 163 encyclicals issued between then and the death of Leo XIII in 1902 were addressed only to specific groups of bishops (usually those of one country). With Pius XII, a new and more troubling trend got under way: increasingly, encyclicals were written, not to the pope's brothers in the episcopate but to all and sundry. Thus, John XXIII wrote *Mater et Magistra* 'to the clergy and faithful of the entire Catholic world', and Paul VI cast his net even wider, writing *Ecclesiam Suam* and *Populorum Progressio* not only to Catholics but to 'all men of good will'. Finally, the present pope addresses his encyclicals not to half the human race but to 'all men and women of good will'. I describe this tendency for the bishop of Rome to address, not his brother bishops, but the human race, as 'troubling' because it is one more symptom of dangerously inflated papal power.

In January 1992, the London *Tablet* reported a discussion on BBC radio in which Brian Wicker, a Catholic lay theologian, said that he could see no reason why Vatican diplomats should not be lay people. The pronuncio,

Archbishop Barbarito, replied that this suggestion betrayed an ignorance of a nuncio's duties. Diplomats, he said, acted as an extension of the pope's duty and mission to the bishops, and, 'You cannot expect a layman to have the power to tell the bishops what to do or what not to do.'

Without in any way wishing to suggest that there are no circumstances in which a pope might properly issue instructions to his brother bishops, to imagine that telling them what to do or not to do is a *normal* exercise of papal office is to fall victim to just that massive distortion of Catholic life and teaching with which the First Vatican Council threatened the church in practice, if not in theory, and from which the Second Vatican Council set it free, in theory if not yet in practice.

In other words, Archbishop Barbarito's casual remark betrayed a mentality which finds nothing strange about a situation in which the pope, who sometimes seems these days to be almost the only authoritative teacher in the church, tells other bishops what to do and not to do while addressing letters, on important subjects, over their heads to the church and world at large.

It might be suggested that the best way to deal with this aspect of a much larger problem threatening the health and balance of Catholic Christianity would be to hope that the next pope would make a self-denying ordinance and initiate a *moratorium* in the publication of encyclicals.

But this would be a pity. Although some encyclicals have done great damage, either in their judgment or in the detail of their wording (confining my remarks to the twentieth century, *Pascendi* and *Humanae Vitae* come to mind), others have been solid and effective instruments of leadership and teaching. It would, I think, be generally agreed that the social encyclicals come in this latter category, along with *Mystici Corporis*, *Divino Afflante*, *Mediator Dei*, *Pacem in Terris*, and *Redemptor Hominis*.

What we need, therefore, is not the abolition of encyclicals but, rather, their adaptation to the circumstances of the church today. Such adaptation (if I were to dream) would include three features. First, instead of encyclicals being an act of papal teaching in isolation from the *magisterium* of the full episcopate, steps might be devised to issue letters from the college of bishops, *sub et cum Petro*, to the church or world. Secondly, whereas at present encyclicals are often 'ghost-written' by an individual theologian whose identity is never officially disclosed, the assistance of a wide range of people, representing the breadth and richness of Catholic scholarship, would be sought. Thirdly, instead of being produced in secret and released (as Newman might have said) like thunder from a clear sky, they would be written, as it were, in public, and in a manner responsive to opinion and experience throughout the church.

This dream may seem to some a fantasy, but it is a fantasy with solid precedent. During the past decade, the bishops of the United States have produced three joint pastoral letters in something like the way that I have indicated. 'The Challenge of Peace', 'Economic Justice for All', and 'Called to be One in Christ Jesus', each went through several published drafts over a period of four or five years, before the final version was arrived at (in the case of the last named, on the ministry of women, the process is not yet complete). That, in each case, the process provoked not only discussion but disagreement was to be expected, and is to be welcomed rather than deplored: adult education works that way.

I am not, of course, suggesting that the American procedures could be adopted, simply as they stand, by the universal church; the episcopate is far too numerous, and the church too culturally diverse, for this to be practicable. But it does seem to me, as a non-American sometimes critical of American Catholicism, that these pastoral letters provide a good model for the kind of reform which would make encyclicals both more responsive to the letter and the spirit of the recent Council, and more effective and constructive instruments of teaching, thereby facilitating the reception which Paul VI, in the audience mentioned earlier, sought for his first contribution to the genre: 'We would like to hope that this pontifical and pastoral message of ours will meet with a favourable reception from the great Catholic family.'

Nicholas Lash

Contributors

GREGORY BAUM was born in Berlin in 1923; since 1940 he has lived in Canada. He studied at McMaster University, Hamilton; Ohio State University; the University of Fribourg and the New School for Social Research, New York. He is now Professor of Theology and Social Ethics at McGill University, Montreal. He is editor of *The Ecumenist*; his books include *Religion and Alienation* (1975), *The Social Imperative* (1978), *Catholics and Canadian Socialism* (1980), *The Priority of Labor* (1982), *Ethics and Economics* (1984) and *Theology and Society* (1987).

Address: McGill University, 3520 University St, Montreal H3A 2A7.

EMIL POULAT was born in Lyons in 1920; he is a sociologist and historian of Catholicism. He was co-founder in 1964 of the Group for the Sociology of Religion and in 1965 of *Archives de Sociologie des religions*. His works include *Histoire, dogme et critique dans le crise moderniste* (1962, 1969); *Catholicisme, Democratie et Socialisme* (1977); *Eglise contre Bourgeoisie* (1977); *Liberté, laicité* (1988).

Address: 14–18 rue de Bièvre, F-75005 Paris, France.

HELMUT PEUKERT was born in Gablonz, Czechoslovakia in 1934. He studied philosophy, pedagogics and theology at the universities of Tübingen, Munich, Innsbruck and Münster, gaining his doctorate in theology in 1976 under J. B. Metz and Karl Rahner, and his Habilitation in educational sciences in 1985. Since 1986 he has been a professor in the University of Hamburg. His publications include: *Diskussion zur 'politischen Theologie'* (1969); *Wissenschaftstheorie – Handlungstheorie – fundamentale Theologie* (1976); *Fundamentaltheologie* (1984); *Über die Zukunft vom Bildung* (1984); *Bildung und Vernunft* (1993), together with articles on epistemology, practical philosophy, the basis of the humanities, critical theory and the philosophy of education.

Address: Innocentiastrasse 56, D 2000 Hamburg 13, Germany.

CHRISTOPH THEOBALD was born in Cologne in 1946, became a Jesuit in France in 1978 and was ordained priest in 1982. He is Professor of

Fundamental Theology and Dogmatics in the Faculty of Theology at the Sèvres Centre in Paris and editor of *Recherches de Science Religieuse*, for which he writes a bulletin on systematic theology (God and the Trinity). He has written on the history of modern theology and systematic theology; his books and articles include *Maurice Blondel und das Problem der Modernität. Beitrag zu einer epistemologischen Standortbestimmung zeitgenössischer Fundamentaltheologie*, Frankfurter theologische Studien 35, 1988; 'La foi trinitaire des chrétiens et l'énigme du lien social. Contribution au débat sur la "théologie politique"', in *Monotheisme et Trinité*, Facultés universitaries Saint-Louis, Brussels 1991.

Address: 15 rue Monsieur, 75007 Paris.

JOHN MILBANK has been lecturer in theology at the University of Cambridge since October 1991. Previously, he was Maurice Reckitt teaching fellow at Lancaster University from 1983–1991. He has written *Theology and Social Theory: Beyond Secular Reason*, Oxford 1990, and *The Religious Dimension in the Thought of Giambattista Vico* (2 vols.), New York 1991–2.

Address: The Divinity School, St John's Street, Cambridge CB2 1TW, England.

WERNER JEANROND was born in Saarbrücken in 1955. He studied theology, philosophy and German at the universities of Saarbrücken, Regensburg and Chicago, and since 1981 has taught systematic theology at Trinity College, Dublin. He is a member of the editorial board of *Concilium*. His publications include *Text and Interpretation as Categories of Theological Thought*, Dublin and New York 1988, and *Theological Hermeneutics: Development and Significance*, London and New York 1991; with Jennifer L. Rike he has edited *Radical Pluralism and Truth: David Tracy and the Hermeneutics of Religion*, New York 1991.

Address: School of Biblical and Theological Studies, Trinity College, University of Dublin, Dublin 2, Ireland.

ANNE FORTIN-MELKEVIK was born in Quebec in 1957 and studied theology there. She gained a doctorate in religious anthropology and history of religions at the Sorbonne and a doctorate in theological science at the Institut Catholique de Paris in June 1991. The title of her thesis was 'Towards a Rational Theory of Hermeneutics in Theology'. Since then she has taught fundamental theology at the Faculty of Theology of the Université Laval, Quebec. She has written articles in the fields of fundamental ethics and hermeneutics for *Le Supplément*, and her

'Herméneutique du rapport philosophie-théologie' will appear in *Laval théologique et philosophique*.

Address: Faculté de Theologie, Université Laval, Quebec, Canada G1K 7P4.

RUDOLF VON THADDEN was born in Trieglaff, Pomerania, in 1932. He studied history, theology and Romance languages and literature in Tübingen, Paris and Göttingen; in Göttingen he gained his Promotion with *Die brandenburgisch-preussischen Hofprediger im 17. und 18. Jahrhundert*, Berlin 1959, and his Habilitation with *Restauration und napoleonisches Erbe. Der Verwaltungszentralismus als politisches Problem in Frankreich*, Wiesbaden 1972. Since 1968 he has been Professor of Modern History in Göttingen, since 1983 Associate Director of Studies at the École des Hautes Études in Science Sociales in Paris, and since 1985 a member of the praesidium of the German Evangelischer Kirchentag. His most recent book is *Weltliche Kirchengeschichte. Ausgewählte Aufsätze*, Göttingen 1989.

Address: Seminar für Mittlere und Neuere Geschichte der Universität, Platz der Göttinger Sieben 5, 3400 Göttingen, Germany.

JUAN CARLOS SCANNONE is a Jesuit. He was born in Buenos Aires in 1931, and gained a degree in theology from the University of Innsbruck and a doctorate in philosophy from the University of Munich. He is Vice-Rector of the faculties of philosophy and theology in the University of San Miguel, Argentina, and has been visiting professor in the Universities of Frankfurt and Salzburg, the Munich Hochschule für Philosophie and the Philosophisch-theologische Hochschule in Frankfurt. His most recent publications are *Evangelización, cultura y teología*, Buenos Aires 1990; *Nuevo punto de partida en la filosofía latinoamericana*, Beunos Aires 1990; *Weisheit und Befreiung. Volkstheologie in Lateinamerika* Düsseldorf, forthcoming.

GIOVANNI TURBANTI studied in the universities of Florence and Urbino, gaining his degree in church history in Florence with a thesis on 'The Vatican II Debate on the Moral Problem of Law'. After working for a number of years at the Institute of Religious Sciences in Grosseto, he is doing doctoral research at the Institute of Religious Sciences in Bologna and working with the international research team there which is producing the history of the Second Vatican Council.

Address: via Calvari 7/4, 40 122 Bologna, Italy.

JEAN-LOUIS SCHLEGEL was born in 1946. He studied linguistics, philosophy and theology and now works at Editions du Seuil. He is one of the chief editors of the journal *Esprit* and also teaches sociology of religion and social philosophy at the Institut catholique de Paris. He has written a number of articles in various journals about the situation of religion in modern societies and has translated into French the works of J. B. Metz, H. Küng, H. U. von Balthasar, F. Rosenzweig (*The Star of Redemption*), J. Habermas and Carl Schmitt.

Address: 40 rue Jean Rey, 78220 Viroflay, France.

PAUL VALADIER was born in 1933, entered the Society of Jesus in 1953 and was ordained priest in 1965. After studying philosophy and theology in Paris, he gained a doctorate in 1974 with a thesis on *Nietzsche et la critique du christianisme*, which was subsequently published as a book. From 1970 he has been professor of moral and political theology at the Sèvres Centre (the Jesuit faculty in Paris), and was dean of the faculty from 1974 to 1980. He was also senior editor of the Journal *Études* from 1981 to 1989. Since 1990 he has been a professor at the Catholic University of Lyons. His publications include: *Essais sur la modernité. Nietzsche et Marx*, 1974; *Un christianisme au présent*, 1975; *Nietzsche l'athée de rigueur*, 1975; *Des repères pour agir*, 1977; *Jésus-Christ ou Dionysos. La foi chrétienne en confrontation avec Nietzsche*, 1979; *Agir en politique. Décision morale et pluralisme politique*, 1980; *L'Eglise en procès. Catholicisme et société moderne*, 1987; *Inévitable morale*, 1990; *Lettres à un chrétien impatient*, 1991.

Address: 35, rue de Sèvres, 75006 Paris, France.

PAUL BLANQUART was born in the north of France in 1934. A sociologist and philosopher, he has taught at the Institut Catholique in Paris and the Université Paris XII, run a political weekly, and been director of the Centre de création industrielle at the Centre Beaubourg in Paris. He now trains people to be in charge of social development work in disaster-stricken areas of France, urban and rural. He has written a number of articles, and on questions relating to the topic discussed here he has recently contributed to three collected works edited by René Luneau: *Le retour des certitudes*, Paris 1987; *Le rêve de Compostelle*, Paris 1989; *Les rendez-vous de Saint-Domingue*, Paris 1991. See also 'L'avenir d'une déliaison', *Autrement* 127, February 1992, in *Dieux en sociétés*, 92–104.

Address: 15, rue de l'Asile Popincourt, 75011 Paris.

Members of the Advisory Committee for Fundamental Theology

Directors

Claude Geffré OP	Paris	France
Jean-Pierre Jossua OP	Paris	France

Members

Gregory Baum	Montreal, Quebec	Canada
Alfonso Alvarez Bolado SJ	Madrid	Spain
Maurice Boutin	Montreal, Quebec	Canada
Bertrand de Clercq OP	Louvain	Belgium
Joseph Comblin	Serra Redonda	Brazil
Etienne Cornélis	Nijmegen	The Netherlands
Richard Cote	Ottawa, Ontario	Canada
Iring Fetscher	Frankfurt/Main	Germany
Francis Fiorenza	Hyattsville, Md.	USA
José Fondevila SJ	Barcelona	Spain
Heinrich Fries	Munich	Germany
Pierre Gisel	Lausanne	Switzerland
Bernard Lauret	Paris	France
Italo Mancini	Urbino	Italy
Sallie McFague	Nashville, Tenn.	USA
Andreas van Melsen	Nijmegen	The Netherlands
Johann-Baptist Metz	Münster	Germany
Christopher Mooney SJ	Fairfield, Conn.	USA
Francis O'Farrell SJ	Rome	Italy
Raimundo Panikkar	Santa Barbara, Ca	USA
Helmuth Rolfes	Kassel	Germany
Ludwig Rütti	Lengerich	Germany
Giuseppe Ruggieri	Catania	Italy
Juan-Carlos Scannone SJ	San Miguel	Argentine
Norbert Schiffers	Ratisbonne	Germany
Heinz Schlette	Bonn	Germany
Jon Sobrino	San Salvador	El Salvador
Robert Spaemann	Stuttgart-Botnang	Germany
David Tracy	Chicago, Ill.	USA
Roberto Tucci SJ	Vatican City	Italy

Members of the Board of Directors

Founders

A. van den Boogaard	Nijmegen	The Netherlands
P. Brand	Ankeveen	The Netherlands
Y. Congar OP	Paris	France
H. Küng	Tübingen	Germany
K. Rahner SJ	Innsbruck	Austria
E. Schillebeeckx OP	Nijmegen	The Netherlands

Directors/Counsellors

Giuseppe Alberigo	Bologna	Italy
Willem Beuken SJ	Louvain	The Netherlands
Leonardo Boff	Petrópolis	Brazil
Julia Ching	Toronto	Canada
John Coleman SJ	Berkeley, CA	USA
Christian Duquoc OP	Lyons	France
Virgil Elizondo	San Antonio, TX	USA
Sean Freyne	Dublin	Ireland
Claude Geffré OP	Paris	France
Norbert Greinacher	Tübingen	Germany
Gustavo Gutiérrez	Lima	Peru
Hermann Häring	Nijmegen	The Netherlands
Bas van Iersel SMM	Nijmegen	The Netherlands
Werner Jeanrond	Dublin	Ireland
Jean-Pierre Jossua OP	Paris	France
Nicholas Lash	Cambridge	Great Britain
Kabasele Lumbala	Mbuji Mayi	Zaïre
Mary-John Mananzan OSB	Manila	Philippines
Norbert Mette	Münster	Germany
Johann-Baptist Metz	Münster	Germany
Dietmar Mieth	Neustetten	Germany
Jürgen Moltmann	Tübingen	Germany
Alphonse Ngindu Mushete	Kasai Oriental	Zaïre
Aloysius Pieris SJ	Gonawala-Kelaniya	Sri Lanka
David Power OMI	Washington, DC	USA
James Provost	Washington, DC	USA
Giuseppe Ruggieri	Catania	Italy
Paul Schotsmans	Louvain	Belgium
Lisa Sowle Cahill	Chestnut Hill, MA	USA
Miklós Tomka	Budapest	Hungary
David Tracy	Chicago, IL	USA
Marciano Vidal	Madrid	Spain
Knut Walf	Nijmegen	The Netherlands
Anton Weiler	Heelsum	The Netherlands
Christos Yannaras	Athens	Greece

General Secretariat: Prins Bernhardstraat 2, 6521 AB Nijmegen, The Netherlands
Secretary: Mrs E. C. Duindam-Deckers